RECIPE NOTES

Butter should always be unsalted.

Pepper is always freshly ground black pepper, unless otherwise specified.

All herbs are fresh and parsley is flat-leaf, unless otherwise specified.

Vegetables and fruits are assumed to be medium size, unless otherwise specified.

Eggs are assumed to be medium size, unless otherwise specified.

Milk is always full-fat, unless otherwise specified.

Garlic cloves are assumed to be large; use two cloves if yours are small.

Ham means cooked ham, unless otherwise specified.

Prosciutto refers exclusively to raw, dry-cured ham, usually from Parma or San Daniele in northern Italy.

Sugar is always granulated white sugar, unless otherwise specified.

Cooking and preparation times are for guidance only, as individual ovens vary. If using a convection oven, follow the manufacturer's directions concerning oven temperatures.

Some recipes include raw or very lightly cooked eggs. These should be avoided particularly by the elderly, infants, pregnant women, convalescents, and anyone with an impaired immune system.

All spoon measurements are level, unless otherwise specified.
1 teaspoon = 5 ml
1 tablespoon = 15 ml

THE SILVER SPOON
FOR CHILDREN

FAVORITE ITALIAN RECIPES

CONTENTS

LUNCHES & SNACKS

PASTA & PIZZA

MAIN COURSES

BAKING & DESSERTS

COOKING THE
ITALIAN WAY

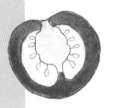

Most people love eating Italian food, so it's fantastic if you know how to cook it! We have chosen forty recipes from *The Silver Spoon*, the best-selling cookbook that can be found in almost every Italian family's kitchen. We've adapted the recipes so they are very easy for you to follow. These are traditional Italian recipes that have been handed down from generation to generation, so with this book you can imagine that you are in a kitchen in Italy, learning how to cook the Italian way.

Over the centuries, Italians have discovered exactly how to mix a few simple, good-quality ingredients to make meals that are full of flavor. For instance, you can make a delicious sauce for pasta with just a few basic items such as good-quality canned tomatoes, fresh basil, garlic, and a good olive oil. The recipes in this book will help you learn some key skills and techniques used in any kitchen, not just Italian ones: you will learn how to use a small sharp knife (which is essential if you are going to do some proper cooking!), how to prepare vegetables, how to cook pasta, even how to make your own pizza dough from scratch.

Cooking isn't just about making something good to eat: by following the recipes, you will practise some maths (measuring, sharing), reading (the recipes as well as lots of fun bits of information along the way), geography (you will learn some interesting facts about Italy), and perhaps even art (you could try drawing the food you have cooked, just like Harriet has done for the recipes in this book).

All the recipes in *The Silver Spoon for Children* have been tested by children—if you're aged nine or ten or older, you should be able to follow most of the recipes by yourself, with some occasional help from an adult. But do always remember to check with an adult before you begin and make sure that there is someone with you when you use a sharp knife, the oven, or electrical equipment like a food processor. If you're younger than nine you will need help from an adult, or an older brother or sister. Harriet's drawings will help you along the way.

So make some time to have fun in the kitchen preparing these delicious Italian dishes. You can then enjoy sharing your meal with family and friends—just like the Italians!

COOKING SAFELY

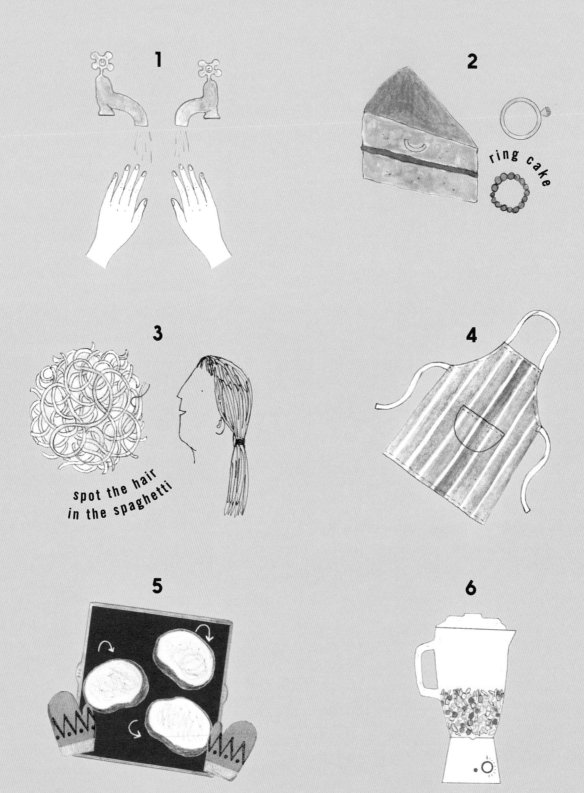

1

2

ring cake

3

spot the hair
in the spaghetti

4

5

6

Cooking is a little like reading: Once you have learnt the basics, the rest will begin to fall into place. You will learn some very useful techniques and skills in this book, but there are a few things to think about before you start, most of which I'm sure you will already know:

1 Wash your hands before you start cooking, and use a hand towel or paper towel instead of drying them on your clothes. You will also need to wash your hands after handling any raw meat or fish.

2 Take off any jewelry you're wearing on your hands. You don't want to bite into a piece of cake and find yourself munching on a ring!

3 If you have long hair, it's a good idea to tie it back. No one likes eating food with hair in it.

4 Put on an apron to protect the food you're preparing from any dirt on your clothes (and to keep your clothes clean, too!).

5 Always wear oven mitts when you're putting anything into the oven or taking anything out of the oven. You will also need to wear oven mitts when you're putting food under a hot broiler or turning over food halfway through cooking.

6 Always ask an adult to help when you use the oven or a food processor, or when you're draining pasta in a colander.

7 And the most important thing: Always ask an adult before you start cooking.

EQUIPMENT & UTENSILS

1

2

3

4

5

6

7

8

You don't need much equipment to make the recipes in this book, but it helps to have the following:

1 SMALL SHARP KNIFE

One of the first skills all budding chefs should learn is how to use a knife properly. It's also good to learn to choose the right knife for each job. A paring knife is a good place to start—this is a small sharp knife suitable for trimming and chopping fruits and vegetables.

Did you know that a blunt knife is more dangerous than a sharp one? You have to apply a lot of pressure to cut through something with a blunt knife, but a good sharp knife glides through food easily, with less risk of it slipping. The two main cutting techniques are the bridge and the claw techniques (see pages 12–13). Once you have mastered these, you will be able to cut most things safely, but always ask an adult before you use a sharp knife.

2 CUTTING BOARDS

These can be plastic or wood. Keep them clean by scrubbing them with hot water and washing-up liquid. Always wash them particularly carefully after you've put raw meat, fish, or egg on them.

3 WOODEN SPOON

If you haven't got one of these I suggest you save up some pocket money and buy one—every chef needs a wooden spoon for mixing!

4 SAUCEPANS

A couple of pans are all you need, ideally a big one for cooking pasta and a small one for making sauces. If you have a medium sized one as well, even better!

5 KITCHEN SCISSORS

When you use kitchen scissors to cut food like fresh herbs, always keep your fingers well away from the edges of the blades so that you don't accidentally cut yourself.

6 GARLIC CRUSHER

Garlic is small and can be tricky to chop. A crusher is easy to use: put a peeled garlic clove inside the cup of the crusher, then use both hands to close the crusher, and push hard to squeeze the garlic out. Use a table knife to scrape the garlic off the crusher.

7 FOOD BLENDER OR PROCESSOR

For some recipes, it does help if you have a food blender or processor, but if you don't have one perhaps you could borrow one from a friend. Always ask an adult to help you use a food blender, as it has a very sharp blade in the bottom. Make sure to stay away from the sharp blade, just like you would when using a sharp knife.

8 PESTLE AND MORTAR

A pestle and mortar are fun to use: you pound food in the mortar (the bowl) with the pestle (the heavy stick). If you don't have one, you can use the end of a wooden rolling pin to bash food in a small plastic or wooden bowl instead.

TECHNIQUES

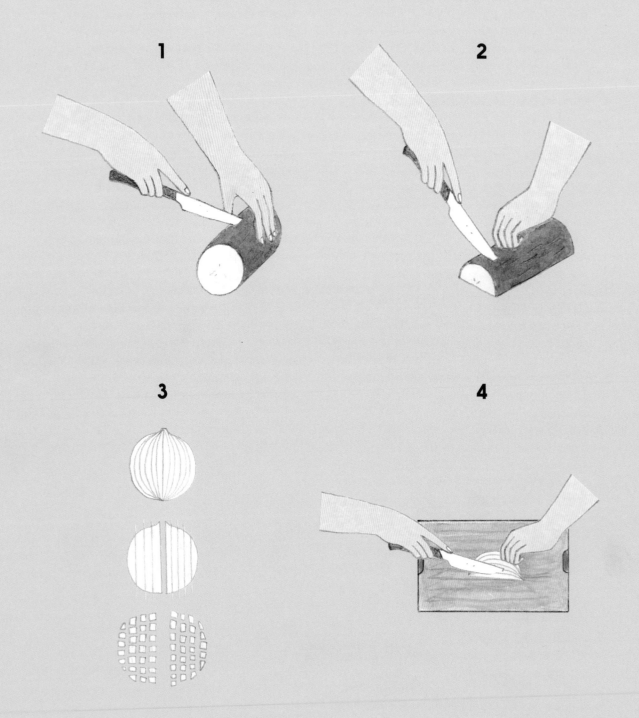

1 BRIDGE CUTTING TECHNIQUE

Hold the piece of food you want to cut by forming a bridge with your thumb on one side and your index finger on the other. Hold the knife in your other hand with the blade facing down, guide the knife under the bridge, and cut through the food. For some soft items such as tomatoes it may be easier to puncture the tomato skin with the point of the knife first before cutting.

2 CLAW CUTTING TECHNIQUE

Place the item on the cutting board with its flat side facing down (often you will need to cut it in half first using the bridge technique). Shape the fingers of your left hand into a claw shape, tucking your thumb inside your fingers and tucking your fingertips in away from the blade. If you're left-handed, you need to make the claw with your right hand! Rest the claw on the item to be sliced. Holding the knife in your other hand, slice the item, moving the "clawed" fingers away as the knife gets closer.

3 HOW TO CHOP AN ONION

Put the onion on a cutting board. Carefully holding it in the claw cutting position, cut the pointed end off the onion. Put the onion on the board with the flat end (the end that you have just cut) sitting on the board. Hold the onion using the bridge cutting position. Cut the onion in half. Peel away the dry papery skin. To chop the onion into small pieces, known as dice, make a bridge using your fingers and thumb, and then use the knife to make lots of vertical cuts through the onion from just above the root end to the top. Then switch to the claw technique and cut across the onion the other way to make small dice.

4 HOW TO CUT AN ONION INTO THIN SLICES

Sit one half, flat-side down, on the cutting board. Hold the onion using the claw technique and cut across the onion to make slices.

MORE TECHNIQUES

5

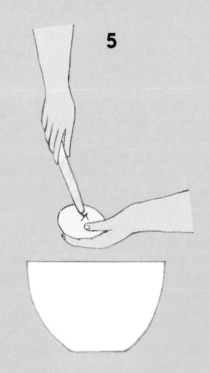

6

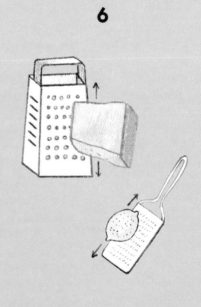

7

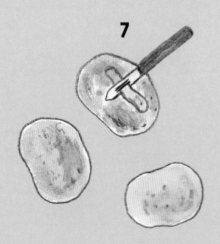

8

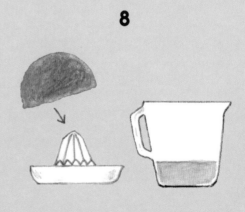

5 HOW TO CRACK EGGS

Hold the egg in one hand, almost cupping it. Hold the egg over a small bowl and hit the middle of the egg with a table knife to crack it. Put the knife down and then put your thumbs into the slit you have just made in the shell. Carefully pull the shell apart and let the egg white and yolk drop into the bowl.

6 HOW TO USE A GRATER

Place the grater on a cutting board and hold it firmly by its handle. Hold the piece of food at its widest end and grate the food by rubbing it up and down the grater. Watch your fingers and knuckles to make sure that they don't get caught on the "teeth" of the grater.

Have you ever noticed that a grater has different sized holes in it? Sometimes you want the food to be grated into big pieces with the big holes, like grated carrots for a salad. Some foods, like Parmesan cheese, are best grated with the small holes—perfect for sprinkling over pasta!

7 HOW TO USE A VEGETABLE PEELER

There are different types of vegetable peelers, so you might need to try a few to see which one you find easiest to handle. Hold one end of the vegetable and rest the other end on a cutting board. Starting halfway down the vegetable, run the peeler down the vegetable away from you. Be careful, as the peeler is sharp! You will need to twist the vegetable as you peel so that you peel all the way around it. Then turn the vegetable up the other way and hold the other end while you peel the other half.

8 HOW TO SQUEEZE JUICE FROM LEMONS AND ORANGES

Cut the lemon or orange in half using the bridge cutting technique (see pages 12–13). If you're feeling strong, pick up half a fruit and squeeze it over a small bowl or jug to catch the juice. Or if you have a squeezer like the one in this illustration, you can put the orange or lemon half on it and push down, twisting the fruit at the same time, to squeeze the juice out of the fruit.

light
meal

buffalo
mozzarella

BUFFALO
MOZZARELLA

LUNCHES & SNACKS

PROSCIUTTO & MELON

Prosciutto (pronounced "pro-shoo-toe") is a delicious kind of ham, and its salty flavor goes very well with the sweet melon in this popular appetizer or antipasto.

Choose small ripe melons for this recipe so that they are easy to cut. Cantaloupe and Honeydew are best, but any type of melon is good. Cantaloupes are round, with pale green bumpy skin and delicious orange flesh inside. Honeydew melons are often bigger and slightly more oval, and have yellowy green skin and pale green flesh.

SERVES	PREPARATION TIME	COOKING TIME
4 people as an appetizer	5 minutes	—

2 small, ripe melons*

—

8–12 slices of prosciutto
(2 or 3 slices for each person)

*To check if the melons are ripe, smell them—they should smell of melon!

PROSCIUTTO & MELON

<table>
<tr><td>STEP 1</td><td>Cut the melons in half using the bridge cutting technique (see pages 12–13). You will need almost to saw through the fruit to cut it, so be careful as you go—always keep your fingers in the bridge position, so that the knife is well away from your fingers. You may need an adult to help you cut the melons.</td></tr>
<tr><td>STEP 2</td><td>Using a dessert spoon, scoop the seeds out of the melons and throw them away.</td></tr>
<tr><td>STEP 3</td><td>Using the bridge cutting technique, cut the melons into quarters by cutting each melon half in half again.</td></tr>
<tr><td>STEP 4</td><td>You can serve the melon on its skin and simply eat it with a knife and fork, or you can use a spoon to scoop out the flesh. Alternatively, you can make the melon easier to eat by using the bridge technique to cut a crisscross pattern in its flesh, but without cutting all the way through the skin.</td></tr>
<tr><td>STEP 5</td><td>You will need four plates. Put two pieces of melon onto each plate, followed by two or three slices of prosciutto.</td></tr>
<tr><td>STEP 6</td><td>Try draping the prosciutto over the melon pieces—you always want to make sure that the food looks good, so that your friends or family enjoy eating it. Serve with a knife and fork or a spoon.</td></tr>
</table>

salty

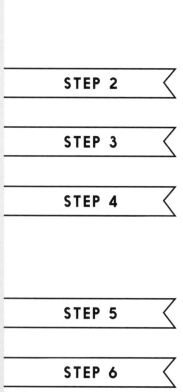

+

sweet

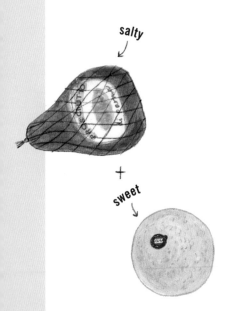

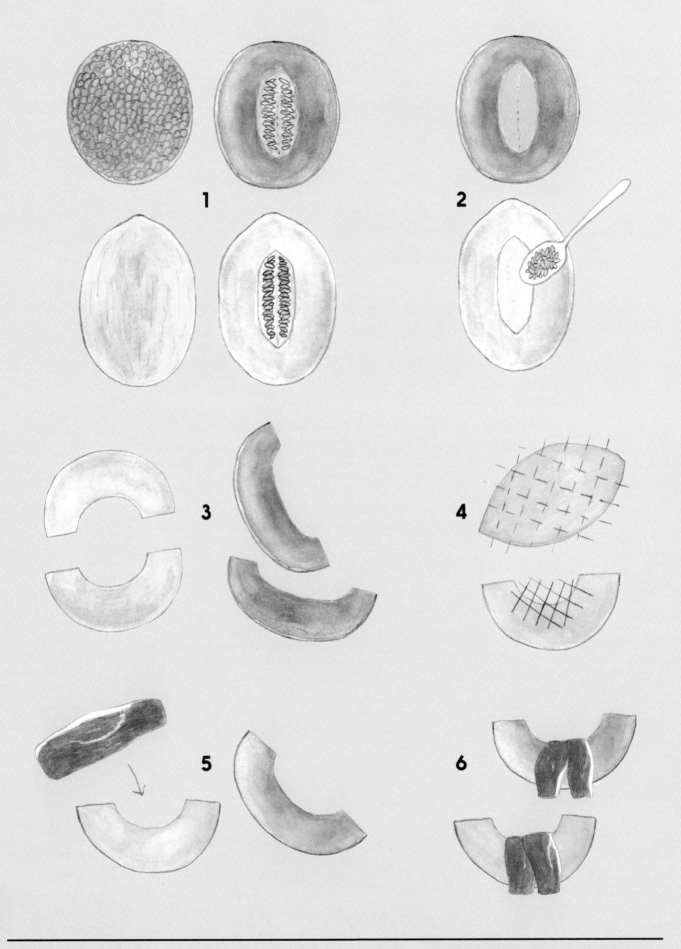

TOMATO BRUSCHETTA

Bruschetta (pronounced "broos-ketta") was originally invented as a good way of using up stale bread by toasting it and adding a range of delicious toppings. The simplest one is made with juicy, ripe tomatoes, and many Italians would say it's the best! You could also try toppings such as mozzarella cheese, basil, ham, or roasted vegetables.

SERVES	PREPARATION TIME	COOKING TIME
4 people as an appetizer	15 minutes	20 minutes

You might need to make more if you want
to eat this for lunch

1 small rustic loaf or 1 small baguette

—

4 tablespoons extra-virgin olive oil for drizzling

—

8 ripe plum tomatoes

—

1 garlic clove

—

freshly ground black pepper (optional)

—

a few fresh basil leaves (optional)

TOMATO BRUSCHETTA

STEP 1

Turn on the oven to 350° F. Using a serrated knife (a knife with a jagged edge) use the claw cutting technique (see pages 12–13) to slice the bread into 8 slices. Try to cut the bread slightly diagonally so that the slices have an oval shape. You might want to ask an adult to cut it for you.

STEP 2

Lay the bread slices flat on a baking tray. Using a spoon, drizzle 2 tablespoons of oil over all the slices—it won't cover all the bread, just drip it over in places.

STEP 3

Wearing your oven mitts, put the baking tray into the oven. After 10 minutes, take the tray out, carefully turn the bread over, and then put back into the oven for another 10 minutes.

STEP 4

The bread should now be a light golden color and crisp. Take the bread out of the oven and rest the tray on a pan stand. Let cool slightly.

STEP 5

For the tomato topping, cut a ripe plum tomato in half lengthwise using the bridge cutting technique (see pages 12–13). Put a tomato half on a cutting board, with its flat side facing down.

STEP 6

Again using the bridge technique, cut the tomato half into long thin strips, then move your fingers into the claw position, and cut the long strips into little pieces. This is called dicing. The diced tomatoes should be in tiny squares, but it doesn't matter if they are different sizes—they will still taste great!

STEP 7

Peel the papery skin away from the garlic clove. Pick up a slice of toasted bread and rub both sides with the garlic. Do the same with the other slices of toasted bread.

STEP 8

Put the toasted bread slices on a big plate, divide the tomatoes among them, and drizzle with the remaining olive oil. If you like, you could sprinkle some black pepper over the top, too, or some fresh basil leaves, torn into small pieces.

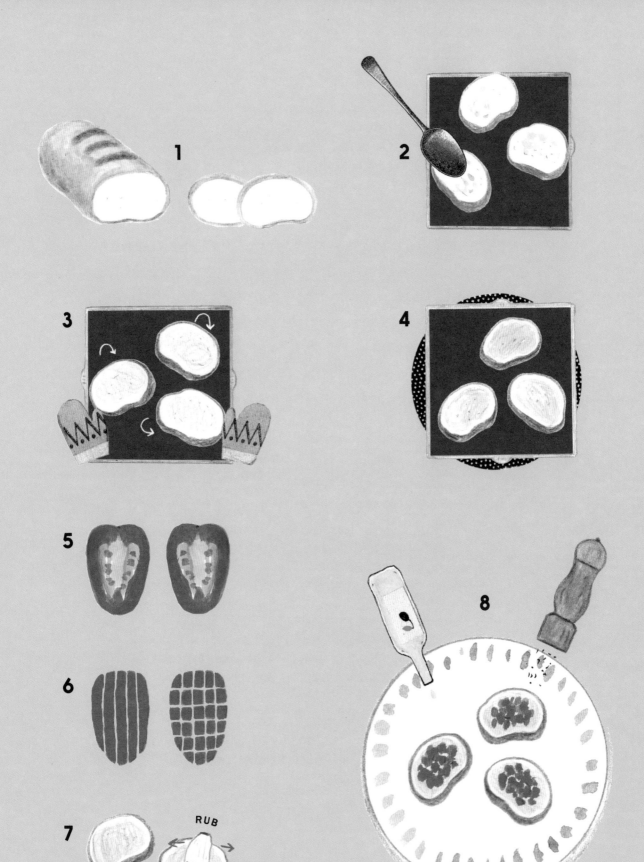

SAUSAGE CROSTINI

Crostini are little toasts with different toppings. This one, with sausage meat and Taleggio cheese, makes a great lunch dish with salad greens. Taleggio is a soft cheese from northern Italy, where people used to leave it in caves in the mountains to ripen. You can have fun crushing the fennel seeds for this recipe, either with a pestle and mortar (see pages 10–11) or with a rolling pin.

SERVES	PREPARATION TIME	COOKING TIME
4	20 minutes	15 minutes

3 good-quality pork sausages

—

1 teaspoon fennel seeds

—

4½ ounces Taleggio cheese, or any other cheese you like that will melt easily

—

8 slices rustic bread

SAUSAGE CROSTINI

STEP 1

Turn on the oven to 350° F. Using kitchen scissors (see pages 10–11), snip the sausages to open the skin and then squeeze the sausage meat into a bowl.

STEP 2

Put the fennel seeds into a mortar and grind with a pestle to crush the seeds, or put the seeds into a small plastic or wooden bowl and crush them with the end of a rolling pin. Stir the crushed fennel seeds into the sausage meat.

STEP 3

Carefully peel the rind away from the cheese and throw the rind away. Break the cheese into small chunks.

STEP 4

Put the cheese into the bowl with the sausage meat and use a spoon or a fork to mix everything together.

STEP 5

Cut the slices of bread in half using the bridge technique (see pages 12–13). Put the bread onto a baking tray (you might need two trays) and spread a layer of sausage mixture onto each slice, like a thick layer of jelly.

STEP 6

Wearing your oven mitts, put the baking tray (or trays) in the oven, and cook for 15 minutes. The bread should be slightly crisp and toasted, the sausage meat will be cooked, and the cheese will have melted.

TALEGGIO CAVES

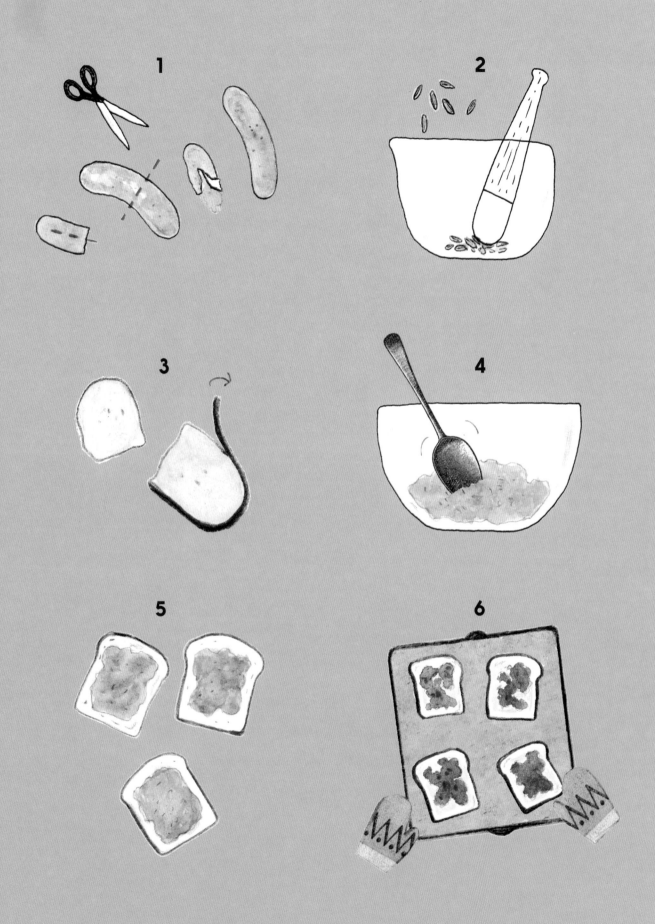

PIZZAIOLA TOASTS

This is a great appetizer or light lunch on a summer's day. You can get everything ready beforehand and then spoon the mixture onto the toasts when you are ready to eat. These are quite messy to eat, so you could put the filling between two pieces of toast to make a sandwich.

SERVES	PREPARATION TIME	COOKING TIME
4	20 minutes	—

2 firm ripe tomatoes

—

2 scallions

—

6 green olives

—

2 fresh flat-leaf parsley sprigs

—

a few fresh oregano leaves

—

1 tablespoon extra-virgin olive oil

—

about 8 slices white bread (or fewer
if the slices are very big)

—

4 ounces mozzarella cheese

PIZZAIOLA TOASTS

STEP 1

Cut the tomatoes in half using the bridge technique (see pages 12–13) and scoop out the seeds with a teaspoon. Using the claw technique (see pages 12–13), cut the tomato flesh into thin strips and then cut each strip into small square pieces, like little dice. Put the small tomato pieces into a bowl.

STEP 2

Using the claw technique, trim the scallions by cutting off the roots and the dark green part of the other ends. Then cut the scallions into thin slices and add to the tomatoes.

STEP 3

Using a rolling pin, carefully squash an olive slightly, so you can open it up and take the pit out. Do this with all the olives.

STEP 4

Using the bridge technique, cut the olives into quarters and add to the tomatoes. Pull the herb leaves off the stalks, then using kitchen scissors (see pages 10–11) snip the parsley and oregano into small pieces. Add half of the herbs and oil to the tomatoes and mix with a spoon.

STEP 5

Toast the bread in a toaster. Using a cookie cutter (about 2⅛ inches in diameter), cut rounds out of the toast—how many rounds you can make will depend on how big your slices of toast are.

STEP 6

Take the mozzarella cheese out of its liquid and tear the cheese into small pieces. Put the rounds of toast onto a big plate. Divide the tomato mixture among the toasts and top with mozzarella. Sprinkle the fresh herbs over the toasts and enjoy!

PANZANELLA SALAD

Like bruschetta (see page 22), panzanella was invented as
a way to use up old bread. Nowadays, Italian cooks often like
to add olives or chopped cucumber, red onion, or scallions to
this traditional salad, so you might like to try adding these, too.

Panzanella is even tastier if you prepare it a few hours before
you want to eat it, so that the bread can absorb the flavor of
the tomatoes. You will need firm, tasty rustic bread with
a coarse texture and really ripe tomatoes with lots of flavor.

SERVES	PREPARATION TIME	COOKING TIME
4	15 minutes	—

6 slices homemade or rustic bread

—

2 tablespoons red wine vinegar

—

4 really ripe and juicy tomatoes

—

freshly ground black pepper

—

6 basil leaves

—

3 tablespoons extra-virgin olive oil

—

olives, chopped cucumber, red onions, or scallions (optional—
you could try adding a handful of each or any of these to the salad)

PANZANELLA SALAD

STEP 1

Cut or tear the crusts off the slices of bread.

STEP 2

Break the bread into small pieces and put into a bowl.

STEP 3

Sprinkle a little red wine vinegar over the bread. This adds a bit of flavor and makes the bread nice and moist.

STEP 4

Coarsely chop the tomatoes into small pieces using the bridge and claw cutting techniques (see pages 12–13).

STEP 5

Add a pinch of freshly ground black pepper to the bread. Tear the basil leaves and sprinkle them over the bread, then drizzle over the olive oil.

STEP 6

Add the tomatoes and any other ingredients you might like to add. Using two forks or a big spoon, mix everything together. If you can, wait a few hours for the flavors to mingle before eating—it will taste even better.

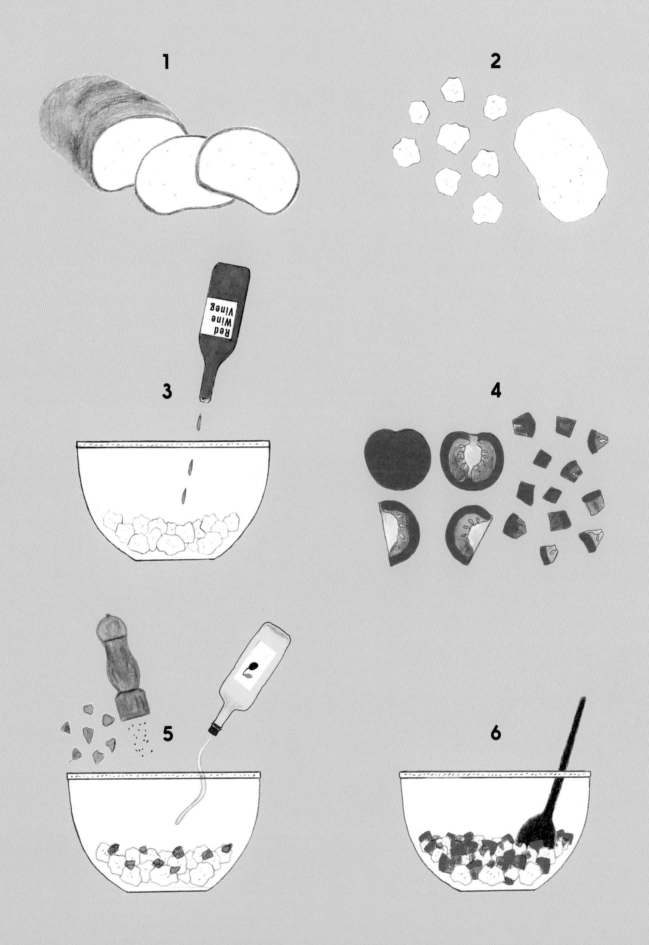

MOZZARELLA & TOMATO SALAD

This simple salad is delicious served with crusty bread to mop up the juices. The recipe originally comes from the island of Capri in southern Italy. That's the same region that pizza comes from, and tomatoes, mozzarella, and basil are also important ingredients in many traditional pizza toppings.

It's best to use really ripe tomatoes for this recipe, so choose them very carefully—they should be deep red and smell like tomatoes! It doesn't matter if your tomato slices aren't all the same shape or thickness, they will still taste delicious. Keep tomatoes in the kitchen, not the refrigerator, so that they continue to ripen and taste good.

SERVES	PREPARATION TIME	COOKING TIME
4	10 minutes	—

4 ripe tomatoes

—

8 ounces mozzarella cheese

—

8 fresh basil leaves

—

2 tablespoons extra-virgin olive oil

MOZZARELLA & TOMATO SALAD

STEP 1

Cut the ripe tomatoes into rings using the bridge technique (see pages 12–13). Try to cut them as thin as you can, but it really doesn't matter if they are not all the same thickness. You may find it easier to first cut the tomatoes in half widthwise, also using the bridge technique. Then place the tomato halves cut side down on a cutting board and slice them into thin strips using the claw cutting technique. This way, you end up with half circles rather than rings.

STEP 2

Take the mozzarella cheese out of its liquid (this liquid helps to keep the cheese fresh). Carefully tear the cheese into pretty pieces. If your mozzarella is very soft, you can almost peel the cheese to make delicate petal shapes.

STEP 3

Sprinkle the tomatoes and cheese on the plate in any way you choose—your plate should have a lovely mixture of red and white on it. Tear the basil leaves and sprinkle them over the top, then drizzle over the olive oil. Keep the salad cool until you are ready to eat.

SUMMER CANNELLINI BEAN SALAD

Cannellini beans are especially popular in a region of Italy called Tuscany. People who live there are sometimes even called mangia-fagioli, or "bean-eaters!" This cannellini bean salad is perfect for a light summer lunch, a picnic, or as a side dish with cooked chicken or chops. This is a great recipe for practicing chopping with a small knife, as you start by dicing the vegetables—this means cutting them into small pieces.

SERVES	PREPARATION TIME	COOKING TIME
4	15 minutes	25 minutes

1 eggplant

—

1 yellow bell pepper

—

2 ripe tomatoes

—

1 garlic clove

—

2 tablespoons extra-virgin olive oil

—

14-ounce can cannellini beans, drained and rinsed

—

1 lemon

—

4 fresh basil leaves

—

1 fresh flat-leaf parsley sprig

SUMMER CANNELLINI BEAN SALAD

STEP 1

Dice the eggplant: Using the bridge technique (see pages 12–13), cut the eggplant in half widthwise and then cut each half in half again lengthwise. Rest the quarters flat side down on a cutting board and, using the bridge technique, cut each quarter into thin strips. Using the claw technique (see pages 12–13) cut each eggplant strip into small pieces.

STEP 2

Dice the bell pepper using the same techniques as for the eggplant: Cut the bell pepper in half and remove the seeds and white part, then cut it into strips. Cut the strips of bell pepper into small pieces.

STEP 3

Then dice the tomatoes in the same way: Cut the tomatoes in half, rest them cut side down on a board, and cut into thin strips. Cut each strip into small pieces.

STEP 4

Peel the papery skin away from the garlic clove. Put the oil in a heavy pan, add the garlic clove, eggplant, and bell pepper, and cook over low heat for about 10 minutes until the bell pepper is slightly soft, stirring occasionally.

STEP 5

Add the tomatoes and beans, cover, and cook very gently for 15 minutes, stirring every now and then.

STEP 6

Take the pan off the heat and use a fork to take out the garlic clove and throw it away.

STEP 7

Carefully grate the yellow peel of the lemon to make lemon zest, keeping your fingers well away from the grater (see pages 14–15). Don't grate the white pith under the yellow skin—it tastes bitter!

STEP 8

Tear the basil leaves into small pieces and snip the parsley leaves into small pieces using kitchen scissors (see pages 10–11).

STEP 9

Spoon the beans and vegetables into a big serving bowl. Sprinkle the lemon zest and herbs over the beans, mix everything together and eat. This dish tastes good warm or cold.

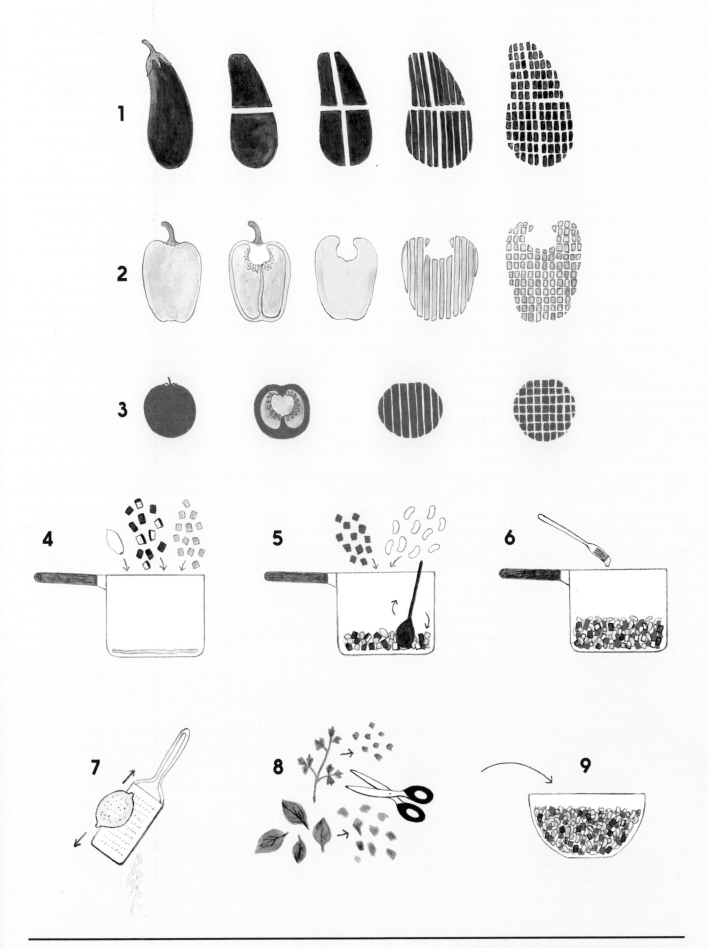

TUNA & BEAN SALAD

You can use canned tuna instead of fresh for this salad, and you can add any fresh ingredients you have in your refrigerator or growing in your yard. This salad tastes so good because you rub garlic around the salad bowl and add crunchy pine nuts and fresh basil leaves. You might like to drizzle a little lemon juice over the top, too. That's the great thing about making salads: You can change the ingredients and make your very own creation!

SERVES	PREPARATION TIME	COOKING TIME
4	20 minutes	5 minutes

1 small thin leek or 1 scallion

—

1 ripe tomato

—

1 small lettuce or 1 head escarole

—

4 small tuna steaks (or 2 x 6-ounce cans tuna in oil, drained)

—

2 tablespoons olive oil

—

1 garlic clove

—

10 fresh basil leaves

—

⅓ cup pine nuts

—

14-ounce can cannellini beans, drained and rinsed

TUNA & BEAN SALAD

STEP 1

Trim the ends off the leek or scallion and then slice it thinly using the claw cutting technique (see pages 12–13).

STEP 2

Using the bridge cutting technique (see pages 12–13), cut the tomato in half and scoop out the seeds using a teaspoon.

STEP 3

Using the claw technique, thinly slice the tomato halves.

STEP 4

Tear or finely slice the lettuce or escarole using the claw cutting technique.

STEP 5

You will need an adult to help you cook the tuna steaks. If you're using canned tuna, go to step 9.) Heat a grill pan or skillet, brush the tuna with a little oil, and put into the pan.

STEP 6

Cook for 2 minutes, use tongs to turn it over, and cook for another 2 minutes—the tuna will still be slightly pink in the middle. You can cook it for longer if you would prefer it not to be too pink.

STEP 7

Cut the garlic clove in half and rub it around the sides of a salad bowl. Tear the basil leaves and put into the bowl together with the pine nuts. Drizzle the oil over the nuts and herbs, and mix well with a spoon.

STEP 8

Add the beans, leek or scallion, tomato, and lettuce or escarole and gently mix everything together.

STEP 9

If you're using canned tuna, break it into chunks and mix them into the beans. If you're using fresh tuna, you can serve the cooked tuna steaks alongside the salad, or slice them into chunks using the bridge technique and mix them in.

pine nuts

Cannellini Beans

TUSCAN MINESTRONE SOUP

Minestrone is a popular vegetable soup, which often has beans, rice, or pasta in it, too. It can be made with just about any of your favorite vegetables, as long as they are chopped up small: It's the small pieces that make the soup a proper minestrone. Sprinkled with grated Parmesan cheese and drizzled with olive oil, it makes a really tasty lunch or supper. Make sure you grate the Parmesan carefully, keeping your fingers well away from the grater!

SERVES	PREPARATION TIME	COOKING TIME
4	25 minutes	45 minutes

2 leeks

—

1 carrot

—

1 celery stalk

—

1 zucchini

—

2 fresh flat-leaf parsley sprigs

—

2 tablespoons olive oil, plus a little extra to drizzle over the finished soup

—

14-ounce can chopped tomatoes

1 fresh rosemary sprig

—

14-ounce can cannellini beans, drained and rinsed

—

4 cups vegetable stock or water (if you are not using fresh stock, use a good vegetable bouillon powder)

—

scant ½ cup long-grain rice

—

1 ounce Parmesan cheese

TUSCAN MINESTRONE SOUP

STEP 1

Using the bridge and claw cutting techniques (see pages 12–13), trim the roots from the bottom and the dark green leaves from the top of the leeks. Then cut the leeks, carrot, celery, and zucchini in half widthwise, then in half lengthwise. Cut each half into thin strips lengthwise. Using the claw technique, cut the thin strips of carrot, celery, zucchini, and leek into small pieces.

STEP 2

Snip the parsley leaves into small pieces using kitchen scissors (see pages 10–11).

STEP 3

Put the oil, carrot, celery, and parsley in a pan, and cook over very low gentle heat for about 10 minutes, stirring every now and then with a wooden spoon.

STEP 4

Add the zucchini, leek, and chopped tomatoes to the mixture and cook for another 10 minutes, stirring every now and then.

STEP 5

Pick the leaves off the sprig of fresh rosemary. Add the beans, rosemary, and stock and bring to a boil.

STEP 6

Add the rice and cook for another 15–20 minutes until the rice is cooked. To check if it's ready, taste a little rice with a teaspoon—remember it will be hot! It should be tender, but still have a little "bite" in the middle.

STEP 7

You will need an adult to help you very carefully ladle half of the soup into a food processor and blend until smooth. Pour back into the pan and stir.

STEP 8

Carefully grate the Parmesan (see pages 14–15) and sprinkle over the top of the soup. Drizzle over some olive oil.

TUNA FRITTATA & GREEN BEANS

Frittata is a type of omelet. It's delicious served hot or cold, making it a great lunch or picnic dish. The first time you make a frittata, you might prefer to serve it just with a salad, but when you are more confident about cooking one, you can try making the beans and tomatoes to go with it, too. You could also try adding other ingredients such as chopped ham or crumbled cheese instead of tuna. If you decide to make both parts of this recipe, make the beans with tomatoes first and leave them to one side while you cook the frittata.

SERVES	PREPARATION TIME	COOKING TIME
4	25 minutes	30 minutes

FOR THE FRITTATA:

1 scallion

—

6 barnyard eggs

—

1 fresh flat-leaf parsley sprig

—

2 tablespoons butter

—

6-ounce can tuna in oil, drained

FOR THE GREEN BEANS WITH TOMATO:

1 scallion

—

1 pound 5 ounces green beans

—

6 green olives

—

1 tablespoon extra-virgin olive oil

—

1 garlic clove

—

14-ounce can chopped tomatoes

—

6 fresh basil leaves

—

freshly ground black pepper

TUNA FRITTATA & GREEN BEANS

STEP 1

Using the bridge and claw cutting techniques (see pages 12–13), trim the roots from the bottom and dark green leaves from the top of the scallion and then finely slice the scallion.

STEP 2

Crack the eggs into a bowl (see pages 14–15) and whisk lightly with a fork. Using kitchen scissors, snip the parsley into pieces (see pages 10–11) and add to the eggs. Turn the broiler onto high.

STEP 3

Melt the butter in a skillet and cook the scallion gently over medium heat for 5 minutes until soft. Add the tuna and stir the mixture gently.

STEP 4

Turn the heat up slightly and pour the egg mixture over the tuna and scallion. Move the egg around in the skillet a few times to help it cook, then leave for 2–3 minutes until the bottom of the frittata is cooked.

STEP 5

Wearing your oven mitts, put the pan under the broiler for 2–3 minutes until the egg is cooked all the way through and is golden and bubbly on top. Serve with the green beans with tomato.

STEP 6

For the green beans with tomato: using the bridge and claw cutting techniques (see pages 12–13), trim the roots from the bottom and dark green leaves from the top of the scallion and then finely slice the scallion. Trim the ends off the beans.

STEP 7

Using a rolling pin, carefully squash an olive slightly, so you can open it up and take the pit out. Do this with all the olives.

STEP 8

Half-fill a pan with water. Put the green beans into a steamer or colander and put it on top of the pan, over the water. Cover with a lid. Bring to a boil and steam the beans for 3–4 minutes. Take off the heat.

STEP 9

Put the oil, scallion, and garlic in a pan and cook over low heat for 5 minutes, stirring occasionally.

STEP 10

Using a fork, fish out the whole garlic clove. Add the beans, chopped tomatoes, and olives, and season with a little freshly ground black pepper.

STEP 11

Tear the basil into pieces and add, then simmer over low heat for 2–3 minutes.

Tagliatelle nest

Pizza cutter unicycle

A pizza fit for a Queen

PASTA & PIZZA

ITALY

PIZZA DOUGH

Pizza has been a popular dish in Italy for hundreds of years, and now it is eaten all around the world. Once you have mastered making pizza dough, you can have fun with lots of different toppings—look at pages 64–71 for ideas.

MAKES	PREPARATION TIME	COOKING TIME
2 big pizza bases	1½ hours	—

FOR THE DOUGH:

2 cups strong bread flour or Italian type "00" flour,
plus extra for dusting

—

1 envelope (⅛ ounce) active dry yeast

—

2 tablespoons olive oil, plus extra
for brushing the trays

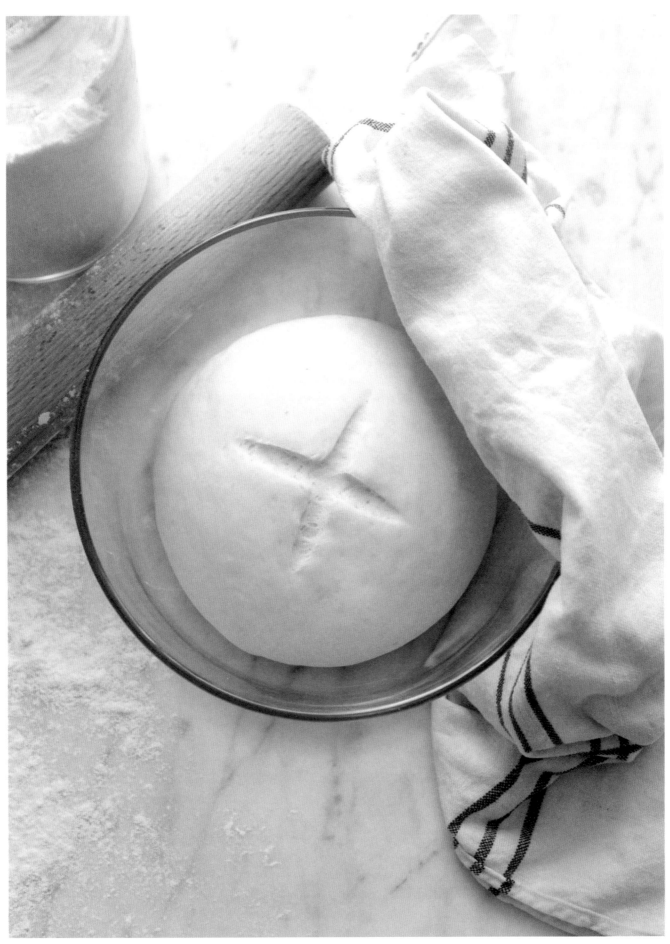

PIZZA DOUGH

STEP 1

You will need ⅓ cup warm water, so first measure ⅓ cup cold water in a measuring cup and then add ⅓ cup hot water. Dip your finger in to test the temperature—it should feel just warm.

STEP 2

Sift the flour into a really big bowl. Sprinkle the dried yeast over the flour.

STEP 3

Make a well—a big hole—in the middle of the flour, deep enough so that you can see the bottom of the bowl. Pour the warm water and olive oil into the well in the flour.

STEP 4

Use a wooden spoon to mix everything to a soft dough.

STEP 5

Sprinkle a little flour over your counter and place the dough onto the flour. Knead the dough by pushing it away from you with the base of your hands and then pulling it back with your fingers. Keep doing this for about 5 minutes until you can stretch the dough like a big piece of elastic.

STEP 6

Wash and dry your bowl. Shape your dough into a big ball, put into the bowl and cover with a clean dish towel. Leave in a warm place for about 1 hour, until it has doubled in size— watch it grow!

STEP 7

Using a pastry brush, brush 2 large baking trays with a little oil or cut 2 pieces of baking parchment to fit the trays.

STEP 8

Sprinkle a little flour over the counter. Take the dough out of the bowl and cut it in half with a table knife.

STEP 9

Flatten each half with your hands and a rolling pin, and shape it into a big round about the size of a large dinner plate, about ¼ inch thick. Do the same with the other half of the dough to make 2 rounds.

STEP 10

Lift the dough onto your baking trays—you may need to ask someone to help you with this! You are now ready to add your toppings to the pizza bases.

Note: Instead of using a bowl, Italians like to sift the flour right onto a counter. It can get a bit messy, but when you have made this pizza dough successfully a few times in a bowl, you might like to try this, too!

PIZZA MARGHERITA

In 1889, when Italy still had a king and queen, Queen Margherita asked a chef to cook her a pizza. He used ingredients that matched the Italian flag: Red tomatoes, white mozzarella cheese, and green basil.

If you like, you can sprinkle some Parmesan cheese over your Pizza Margherita for extra flavor when it comes out of the oven. It's not strictly authentic, but it tastes good!

If you don't have fresh ripe tomatoes, these pizzas will still taste great just using bottled strained tomatoes, which have a lovely flavor.

MAKES	PREPARATION TIME	COOKING TIME
2 big pizzas	1½ hours	20 minutes

2 big pizza bases (see pages 60–63)

—

4–5 tablespoons bottled strained tomatoes

—

4 ripe tomatoes

—

5 ounces mozzarella cheese

—

6 fresh basil leaves, plus a few extra

—

handful of freshly grated Parmesan cheese (optional)

PIZZA NAPOLETANA

Pizza Napoletana, which was invented in Naples, is another traditional topping for pizzas. With their strong salty taste, anchovies are an important ingredient in this pizza, but if you're trying them for the first time and aren't sure whether you like the taste, use only half the amount suggested here.

MAKES	PREPARATION TIME	COOKING TIME
2 big pizzas	1½ hours	20 minutes

2 big pizza bases (see pages 60–63)

—

4–5 tablespoons bottled strained tomatoes

—

4 ripe tomatoes

—

5 ounces mozzarella cheese

—

8 canned anchovy fillets, drained

—

a pinch of dried oregano

SAUSAGE PIZZA

Sausage pizza is not as traditional a topping as those on either Pizza Margherita or Pizza Napoletana, but the sausages and pancetta (pronounced "pan-chetta"), a type of cured bacon, are very tasty along with the rosemary and basil.

MAKES	PREPARATION TIME	COOKING TIME
2 big pizzas	1½ hours	20 minutes

2 big pizza bases (see pages 60–63)

—

7 ounces good-quality sausages

—

2 ounces pecorino cheese

—

freshly ground black pepper

—

4–5 tablespoons bottled strained tomatoes

—

4 ripe tomatoes

—

3½ ounces pancetta slices or cubes

—

1 fresh rosemary sprig

—

a few fresh basil leaves

PIZZA MARGHERITA

STEP 1

Turn on the oven to 400°F. Spread 2–3 tablespoons bottled strained tomatoes over each pizza base using the back of a spoon. Using the bridge and claw cutting techniques (see pages 12–13) cut the tomatoes in half, and then into slices. Divide the tomato slices between the two pizza bases.

STEP 2

Tear the mozzarella into pieces and sprinkle the pieces of cheese over the tomatoes. Tear the basil leaves and sprinkle over the top. You are now ready to bake your pizzas! Using your oven mitts put both pizza trays in the oven. Bake for 15–20 minutes, until the pizza bases are golden and cooked. Tear a few more fresh basil leaves and sprinkle over the top before you serve.

PIZZA NAPOLETANA

STEP 1

Turn on the oven to 400°F. Follow step 1 as for Pizza Margherita. Then tear the mozzarella into pieces and sprinkle the pieces of cheese over the tomatoes.

STEP 2

Tear the anchovies into small pieces and sprinkle them over the top of the pizza, then the oregano. To bake, follow step 2 for Pizza Margherita.

SAUSAGE PIZZA

STEP 1

Turn on the oven to 400°F. Using kitchen scissors (see pages 10–11), snip open the sausage skin and squeeze the sausage meat into a bowl. Grate the pecorino carefully, making sure that your fingers stay well away from the grater (see pages 14–15). Add the grated cheese, season with a little freshly ground black pepper, and mix with a spoon.

STEP 2

Follow step 1 as for Pizza Margherita. Then dot the sausage meat over the tomatoes. Using kitchen scissors, cut the pancetta into small pieces if it's not cubed already, and sprinkle over the sausage meat. Pick the leaves off the sprig of rosemary and tear the basil leaves, sprinkle both over the top of the pizza. To bake, follow step 2 for Pizza Margherita.

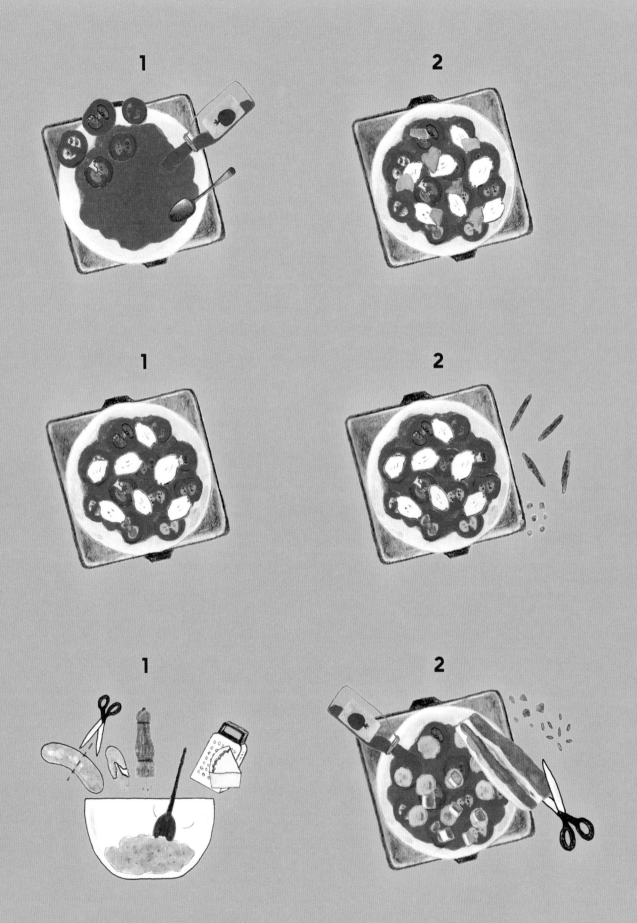

linguine

ravioli

lumache

PASTA

fusilli

penne

cappellini

conchiglie

maccheroni

tagliatelle

rigatoni

farfalle

cappelletti

Pasta is a staple food in Italy. Many people have special big, deep pans with lids they use solely for cooking pasta. You need a big pan because pasta swells and expands as it cooks, and needs plenty of room to move around. If there is not enough room in the pan, the pasta at the bottom will cook quicker than the rest. Some modern pasta pans even have a large colander inside them, ready to drain the pasta when it is cooked.

Pasta comes in all kinds of different shapes and sizes with great names: Short pastas include cappelletti, which means "little hats," and farfalle, which means "butterflies." Long pastas include linguine, which means "little tongues," and capellini, which means "fine hair"—this is the thinnest, wispiest pasta you will ever see.

How many different types of pasta can you think of? How many have you tasted?

Pasta is quick and easy to cook, so it's perfect if you are in a hurry. There are two main types of pasta, fresh and dried. Fresh pasta is usually made with flour and eggs (see pages 74–77) and only keeps for a few days, while dried pasta is usually made just with flour and water, and can be stored for months.

Italians take their pasta very seriously and never overcook it. They boil the pasta until it is cooked but still has a firm texture or "bite" to it, rather than being fully soft. They call this "al dente," which means "to the tooth."

HOW TO COOK DRIED PASTA

STEP 1

Fill the biggest pan you can find three-quarters full with cold water. You will need an adult to help you carry it to the stove. Bring the water to a boil over high heat.

STEP 2

Carefully add the pasta and stir well. Stir occasionally with a long handled spoon to prevent it from sticking. Cook the pasta for 1 minute less than it recommends on the pack, as it's always better that the pasta is slightly undercooked rather than overcooked and soggy. Use a fork to take a piece of pasta from the pan, leave to cool slightly and then test to see if it is ready—it should be cooked but still have a little "bite."

STEP 3

You will need an adult to help you drain the pasta in a colander. Serve the pasta immediately, with the sauce of your choice.

FRESH PASTA DOUGH

You need only two ingredients to make your own fresh pasta—flour and eggs. Italians believe the best flour for pasta-making is a variety called "00" ("doppio zero" or "double zero"), which is very fine and perfect for making a smooth dough. If you can't find this type of flour, try using strong bread flour instead. To give your pasta the best flavor and color, use barnyard eggs from hens that are free to roam and eat grass and corn. Making fresh pasta by hand is great fun. In Italy they make it right on a counter or table, but it's best to start by making it in a bowl first. Once you're confident that you know what you're doing, you could try making it the Italian way. Freshly-made pasta is great with all the different sauces in this book, from tomato sauce (see pages 86–89) to pesto (see pages 94–97).

SERVES	PREPARATION TIME	COOKING TIME
4	1½ hours	—

1¾ cups Italian type "00" flour (or strong bread flour)
—
2 extra-large barnyard eggs

FRESH PASTA DOUGH

STEP 1

Sift the flour into a big bowl or onto a clean counter if you're feeling confident. Make a well—a big hole—in the middle of the flour, deep enough so that you can see the bottom of the bowl.

STEP 2

Crack the eggs into a bowl (see pages 14–15). Pour the eggs into the well in the flour. Use the fingertips of one hand to mix the egg yolks and whites together. Keep stirring slowly: As you stir, the flour will gradually fall into the egg until it is all mixed in.

STEP 3

You can now use both hands to bring all the flour and egg together to make a ball of dough. If you're finding it hard to bring the flour together, wet your hands with some water and then carry on mixing the dough.

STEP 4

Once you have a big ball of dough, start kneading. A great way to knead is to put the dough on a clean floured counter, push it down with the bottom of your hand, then fold the dough over and push down again. Keep turning the dough and pushing and stretching and you will end up with a smooth ball of dough. If your arms start to feel tired, ask someone else to have a go! It will take about 10–15 minutes before the dough is smooth and elastic. If you stop too soon, the dough may tear when you roll it out.

STEP 5

Give yourself and the dough a rest! Wrap the dough in a damp clean dish towel and leave it for 30 minutes to 1 hour.

STEP 6

Now for the rolling. Cut the dough in half—it's easier to roll out 2 smaller pieces. Wrap one half back up in the damp dish towel, to keep it moist. Sprinkle flour over your rolling pin and a clean counter and start to roll one piece of dough. Keep turning the dough so that it doesn't stick to the counter—you may need to lift up the dough and sprinkle more flour underneath as you roll. Roll the pasta dough until it is really thin—about as big as a letter size piece of paper and as thin as possible. If you have a pasta machine, you can use this to roll the pasta out for you.

STEP 7

Use a small sharp knife to cut the fresh pasta. To make tagliatelle, which look like ribbons, cut the dough into long strips about ¼ inch wide. It doesn't matter if they aren't perfectly straight, they will still taste just as good.

STEP 8

Three-quarters fill a large pan with water and bring to a boil. Carefully add the fresh pasta and cook for only 3–4 minutes until it's just done. The pasta should be soft, and should not taste "raw." Ask an adult to help you drain the pasta in a colander.

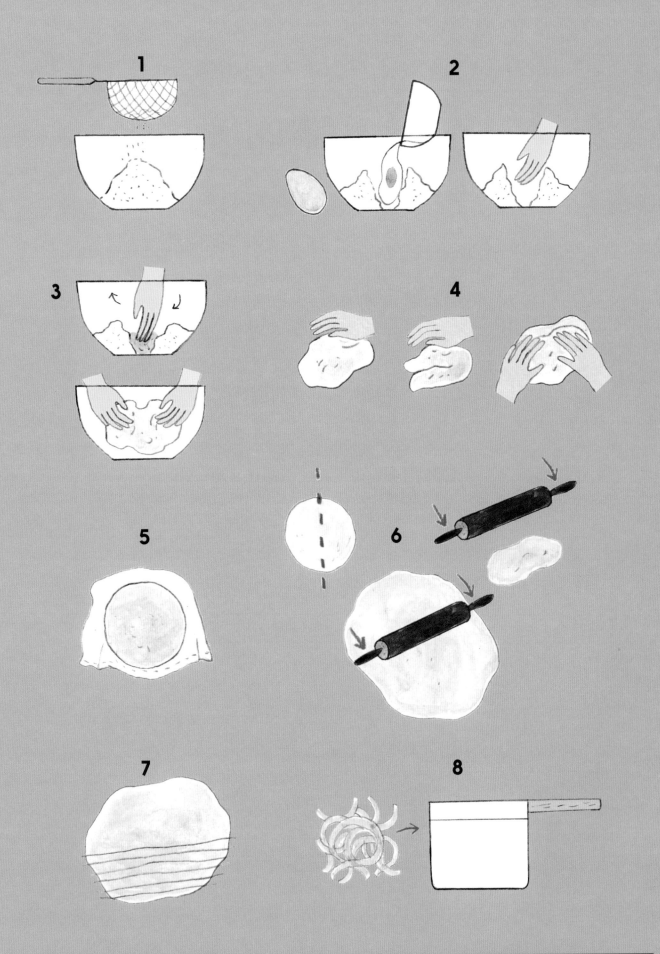

RAVIOLI NAPOLETANA

Ravioli are little pasta shapes that look a bit like miniature pillows, and they can be filled with many different things. Once you've practised this recipe, you can try using different fillings such as cooked pumpkin and ricotta cheese.

SERVES	PREPARATION TIME	COOKING TIME
4	2 hours	5 minutes

1 quantity tomato sauce (see pages 86–89)

FOR THE FRESH PASTA DOUGH:

2¾ cups Italian type "00" flour or strong bread flour

—

3 extra-large barnyard eggs

FOR THE FILLING:

scant ½ cup ricotta cheese

—

3½ ounces cooked ham

—

1 fresh flat-leaf parsley sprig

—

1 barnyard egg

—

3½ ounces mozzarella cheese

—

3½ ounces Parmesan cheese

RAVIOLI NAPOLETANA

STEP 1

Make the tomato sauce by following steps 1 to 5 on pages 88–89 and put to one side. It will be served later with the ravioli.

STEP 2

Make the pasta dough by following steps 1 to 4 on pages 74–77. You need more flour and eggs, but the dough is made in the same way. Cover with a damp dish towel and let rest for 30 minutes.

STEP 3

To make the filling, put the ricotta in a bowl and beat with a wooden spoon. Tear the ham into small pieces and add to the bowl.

STEP 4

Using scissors, snip the parsley leaves into small pieces and add to the ricotta. Crack the egg into a small bowl (see pages 14–15) and whisk with a fork. Tip the egg onto the cheese.

STEP 5

Take the mozzarella out of its liquid and then tear it into small pieces, and add to the ricotta.

STEP 6

Grate the Parmesan, keeping your fingers away from the grater (see pages 14–15), and add to the ricotta. Mix everything together, cover, and keep in the refrigerator until you need it.

STEP 7

Three-quarters fill a pan with water and bring to a boil. Keep it gently simmering, ready to cook the pasta as soon as it is finished.

STEP 8

Take the dough made earlier, cut it in half, and wrap one half back up in the damp dish towel. Always keep pasta dough covered when you're not using it to keep it moist. Roll one half of the pasta dough to the size of a letter size piece of paper, as thinly as you can.

STEP 9

Using a cookie cutter, cut rounds of dough from the sheet. Start at one end and work across. Do this quickly so the pasta doesn't dry out. You will need an even number of rounds—16 would be good.

STEP 10

Spoon a little filling into the middle of 8 of the rounds of pasta. Moisten the edges of the pasta with water, top with the other 8 rounds so you have a total of 8 ravioli. Use your fingers to press the edges of the pasta rounds together, making sure there are no air pockets. This is an important stage—if the ravioli isn't sealed properly, the filling may come out when cooked. Repeat with the other half of pasta dough and the rest of the filling.

STEP 11

Cook the ravioli for 5 minutes or until they rise in the water. Use a slotted spoon to take one out of the pan. Test if it is cooked: The pasta should be soft, and not taste "raw." Serve with tomato sauce.

TAGLIATELLE WITH CREAM, PEAS & HAM

This is a delicious sauce for fresh homemade tagliatelle, but it's also good with dried tagliatelle. This recipe shows how Italians like to eat their pasta sauce—just enough to coat the pasta, not a great big pile of sauce on top!

If you like the flavor of garlic, you could add a crushed garlic clove to the pan with the onion in step two.

SERVES	PREPARATION TIME	COOKING TIME
4	1¾ hours	25 minutes

1 quantity fresh pasta dough (see pages 74–77)
or 14 ounces dried tagliatelle

—

1 onion or 2 scallions

—

2 teaspoons butter

—

2 teaspoons olive oil

—

1¾ cups shelled fresh peas
(or frozen peas if you don't have fresh)

—

2 slices cooked ham

—

scant ½ cup heavy cream

—

1½ ounces Parmesan cheese

TAGLIATELLE WITH CREAM, PEAS & HAM

STEP 1

If you are making fresh pasta, follow steps 1 to 7 on pages 74–77, cutting the pasta into long thin strips to make tagliatelle.

STEP 2

Using the bridge and claw cutting techniques (see pages 12–13), chop the onion or scallions. Heat the butter and oil in a pan over low heat (the butter adds flavor and the oil keeps it from burning). Add the onion and cook gently for 5 minutes until really soft. Stir every now and then with a wooden spoon.

STEP 3

Add the peas, stir to coat them in the buttery juices, and cook for 5 minutes, stirring every now and then with a wooden spoon. Using kitchen scissors, snip the ham into small pieces.

STEP 4

Add the cream to the pan and cook for another 5 minutes, then add the ham.

STEP 5

Three-quarters fill a large pan with water and bring to a boil. Add the fresh tagliatelle and cook for 3–4 minutes until the pasta is just cooked. It should be soft and not taste "raw." If you are using dried pasta, follow the instructions on page 73. Ask an adult to help you drain the pasta in a colander and put it back into the empty pan.

STEP 6

Ladle the sauce over the pasta in the pan. Carefully grate the Parmesan using the small holes on a grater (see pages 14–15), and sprinkle over the pasta. Mix together, and serve right away!

SPAGHETTI WITH TOMATO SAUCE

It's very hard to imagine Italian food without tomatoes, but in fact they have only been grown in Italy since the sixteenth century. At first, people were suspicious of tomatoes because they are related to a poisonous plant called deadly nightshade, but luckily for us, the Italians soon realized how delicious they were. The Italian name for tomato, pomodoro, means "golden apple."

SERVES	PREPARATION TIME	COOKING TIME
4	5 minutes	50 minutes

14-ounce can chopped tomatoes

—

1 teaspoon light brown soft sugar

—

1–2 garlic cloves, depending on how much you like the flavor of garlic

—

14 ounces dried spaghetti

—

10 fresh basil leaves

—

2 tablespoons olive oil

SPAGHETTI WITH TOMATO SAUCE

STEP 1	Put the canned chopped tomatoes into a pan and add the brown sugar.
STEP 2	Squash the garlic cloves slightly with a rolling pin, then peel the garlic, and add to the tomatoes.
STEP 3	Bring the tomatoes up to a gentle simmer, cover, and cook very gently over very low heat for about 40 minutes. Stir the tomatoes occasionally with a wooden spoon.
STEP 4	When your sauce is nearly ready, bring a large pan of water to a boil and cook the spaghetti. (See page 73 for how to cook dried pasta.) Ask an adult to help you drain the spaghetti in a colander and put it back into the pan.
STEP 5	Take the tomato sauce off the heat, tear the basil leaves into small pieces, and add to the sauce with the oil.
STEP 6	Carefully pour or ladle the sauce over the spaghetti, mix together, and serve immediately.

"Pomodoro" means "Golden apple"

Deadly Nightshade
"DO NOT EAT ME"

SPAGHETTI AMATRICIANA

Italians believe that each pasta shape should only be served with certain sauces. Long, thin pasta shapes are usually served with smooth sauces, while short, fat pasta shapes are often served with thicker ones because their holes can carry the pieces in the sauce. In this recipe, the spaghetti is coated in a tomato sauce. When you twist the strands of spaghetti around your fork, you coat the pasta in its sauce and then eat both together.

SERVES	PREPARATION TIME	COOKING TIME
4	10 minutes	1¼ hours

1 fresh red chile

—

3½ ounces pancetta or bacon (cubes or slices)

—

1 onion

—

1 teaspoon olive oil

—

14-ounce can chopped tomatoes

—

14 ounces dried spaghetti

—

freshly ground black pepper

SPAGHETTI AMATRICIANA

STEP 1

The hottest parts of a chile are the pithy white bit and the seeds, so if you take these out you will have the flavor of the chile and a little heat but the sauce shouldn't be too hot. Using the bridge technique (see pages 12–13), cut the chile in half and then use a teaspoon to scrape out the seeds. If you touch the seeds, remember not to touch your eyes—the chile juices will really make them sting! Using the claw technique (see pages 12–13), cut the chile into small pieces. Wash your hands right away!

STEP 2

Using kitchen scissors (see pages 10–11), snip the pancetta or bacon into small pieces, if it's not already cut into cubes.

STEP 3

Use the bridge and claw cutting techniques to chop the onion into small pieces.

STEP 4

Put the olive oil into a heavy pan. Add the pancetta and cook over medium heat for 3 minutes—the pancetta will change from bright pink to a paler pink as it starts to cook. Use a wooden spoon to stir the pancetta around in the pan.

STEP 5

Lower the heat, add the onion, and cook very gently for 10 minutes, stirring every now and then—you want to cook the onions until they are soft.

STEP 6

Add the canned tomatoes and chile. Put the lid on the pan and leave over gentle heat for 40 minutes. You will need to check it every 10 minutes and stir. Add a little more water if the sauce starts to stick to the bottom of the pan. The sauce will become thick and deep red in color as it cooks.

STEP 7

When your sauce is nearly ready, bring a large pan of water to a boil and cook the spaghetti. (See page 73 for how to cook dried pasta.) Ask an adult to help you drain the spaghetti in a colander and put it back into the pan.

STEP 8

Ladle the sauce over the spaghetti in the pan, and mix everything together. Taste the sauce and add freshly ground black pepper. Serve immediately.

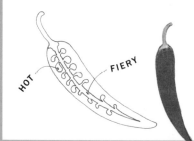

HOT   FIERY

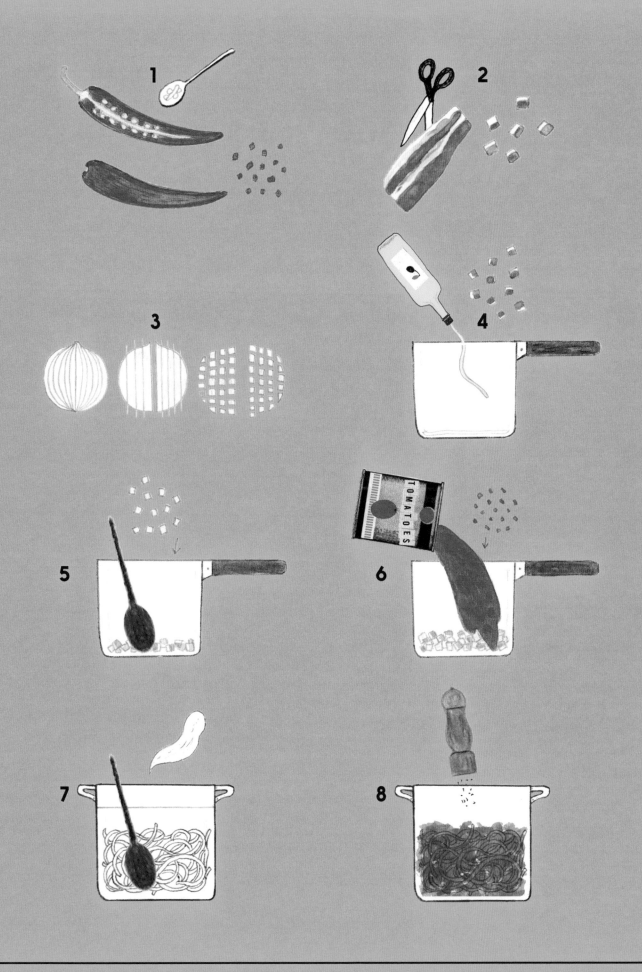

LINGUINE WITH PESTO

Pesto is a bright green sauce from Liguria in northern Italy. Italians usually eat pesto with linguine or trofie pasta, which are little twisted rope shapes, but it's also delicious with steamed green beans or fresh gnocchi (see pages 116–119). Traditionally, pesto is made with a pestle and mortar, which is perfect for pounding the ingredients—borrow one from a friend, if you don't have one. Otherwise, you can also make pesto in a food processor.

SERVES	PREPARATION TIME	COOKING TIME
4	20 minutes	8–10 minutes

2 ounces Parmesan cheese or 1 ounce each
of Parmesan and pecorino

—

½ garlic clove

—

a pinch of salt

—

about ⅓ cup pine nuts

—

about 25 fresh basil leaves

—

scant ½ cup extra-virgin olive oil

—

14 ounces dried linguine

—

freshly ground black pepper

LINGUINE WITH PESTO

STEP 1

Finely grate the cheese (see pages 14–15) and put to one side. Put the garlic and a small pinch of salt (this will make it easier to squash the garlic) into a mortar or food processor, and mash the garlic until it is soft and crushed.

STEP 2

Add the pine nuts and bash until they are broken into small pieces. If you're using a food processor it will only take seconds to whizz the nuts until they are broken into very small pieces, but if you're using a pestle and mortar you might need to take it in turns with friends or family to help you bash everything, to stop your arm from aching!

STEP 3

Add the basil leaves and mash some more. If you're using a pestle and mortar, bash the leaves until they are broken into small pieces. Try to do this quite quickly, to keep the bright green color—the longer you bash, the darker the leaves will go. If you're using a food processor, blend quickly in short bursts.

STEP 4

Spoon the mixture into a bowl, add the cheese, and mix. Then gradually add the oil, until you have a sauce that just drops off your spoon. Hey presto, you've made pesto!

STEP 5

Bring a large pan of water to the boil and cook the linguine. (See page 73 for how to cook dried pasta.) You will need to ask an adult to help you drain the linguine in a colander and tip it back into the empty pan. Add the pesto and carefully stir to coat the pasta with the pesto. Season with freshly ground black pepper, and eat!

some bashing

more bashing

even more bashing

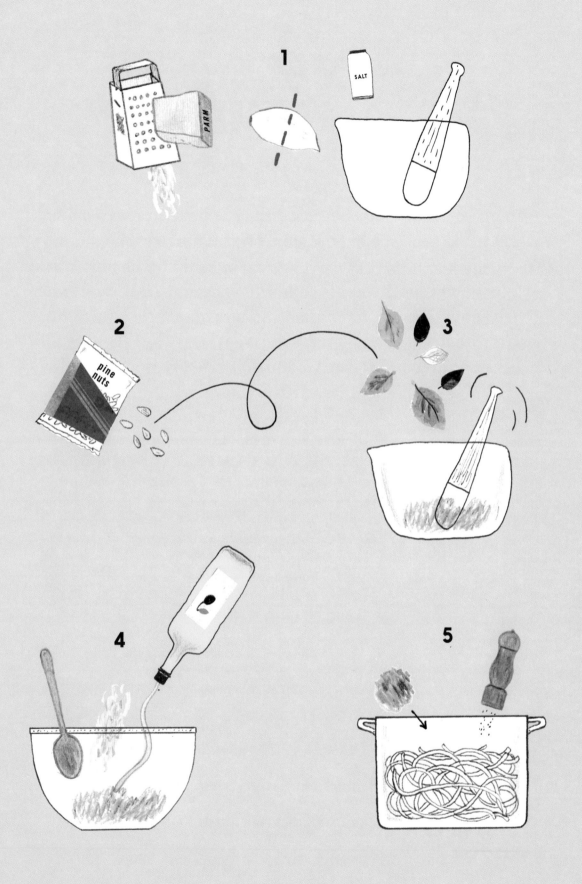

1

2

3

4

5

BAKED MACCHERONI WITH PARMESAN

To make baked maccheroni, you first have to make a very useful white sauce called béchamel (pronounced "bay-sha-mel"). To make it, you start by cooking a combination of butter and flour known as a roux (pronounced "roo"). Once you have learnt how to make béchamel sauce, you can use it in many other dishes, like lasagna (see pages 102–105). This sauce tastes quite plain to start with, so in this recipe, flavor is added with cheese.

SERVES	PREPARATION TIME	COOKING TIME
4	25 minutes	30 minutes

FOR THE BÉCHAMEL SAUCE:

3½ tablespoons sweet butter

—

½ cup all-purpose flour

—

2¼ cups full-fat milk

—

freshly ground black pepper

FOR THE BAKED MACCHERONI:

1 ounce Parmesan cheese

—

1 ounce Cheddar cheese

—

2¾ cups dried maccheroni pasta

BAKED MACCHERONI WITH PARMESAN

STEP 1

Start by grating the Parmesan and Cheddar cheeses, making sure that your fingers stay well away from the grater (see pages 14–15). Set these aside as you will use them later in the recipe.

STEP 2

Now make the sauce. Put the butter in a small pan and melt over gentle heat. You don't want to overheat the butter or let it brown, as this will affect the color and flavor of the sauce.

STEP 3

As soon as the butter has melted, add the flour and cook the mixture over medium heat for 1 minute, stirring constantly with a wooden spoon to make a smooth glossy paste—this is your roux.

STEP 4

Take off the heat, add 4 tablespoons of milk, and stir until the milk is completely mixed in and the mixture is thick and smooth.

STEP 5

Put back on low heat, add a little milk, and stir again. Continue to add milk a little at a time until half of the milk has been added.

STEP 6

Swap your wooden spoon for a whisk and continue to add the rest of the milk. You can add more at a time now, as long as you keep whisking to help prevent the sauce from going lumpy!

STEP 7

Keep the pan on low heat and let the sauce cook very gently for 3–4 minutes, stirring constantly. The sauce will continue to thicken as it cooks. You'll know it's ready when the sauce is thick enough to coat the back of your wooden spoon.

STEP 8

Turn on the oven to 400°F. Bring a pan of water to a boil and cook the maccheroni. (See page 73 for how to cook dried pasta.) Ask an adult to drain the pasta and tip it back into the pan.

STEP 9

Add the Parmesan and Cheddar to the béchamel sauce and season with a little freshly ground black pepper.

STEP 10

Ladle, spoon or pour half of the béchamel sauce over the pasta and use a wooden spoon to mix the pasta and sauce together.

STEP 11

Spoon the pasta into an ovenproof dish about 10 inches square. Spoon the remaining béchamel sauce over the top of the pasta. If you have a ladle, you might find it easier to use this.

STEP 12

Put the ovenproof dish onto a baking tray. Wearing oven mitts, put it into the oven and cook for 20 minutes until golden brown and bubbling. Serve with salad or cooked greens.

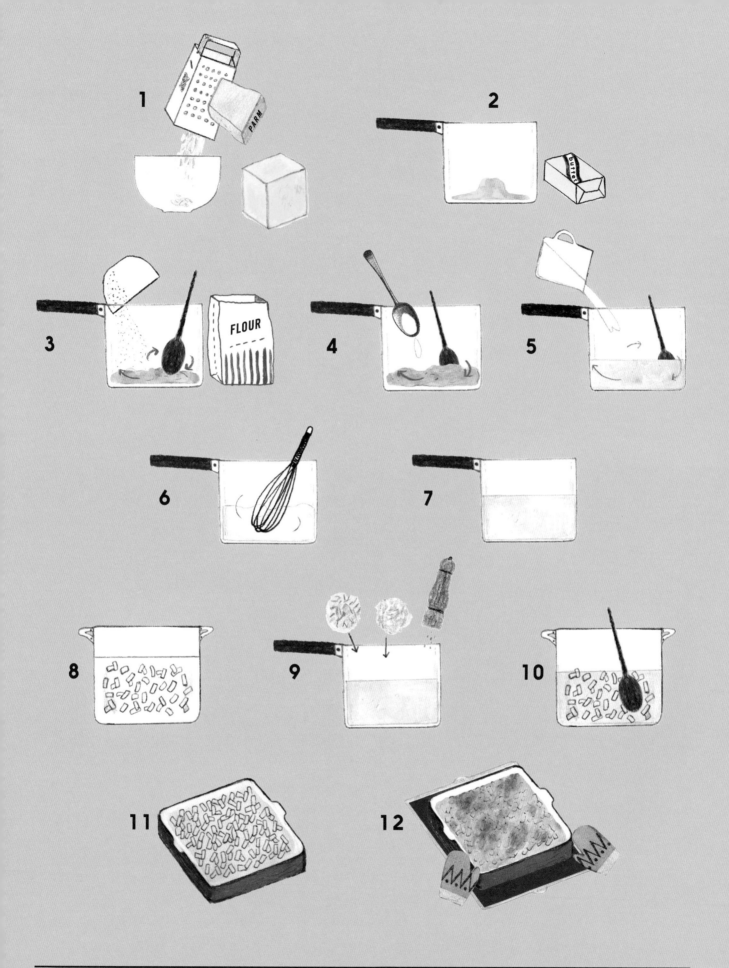

LASAGNA

Lasagna is made up of layers of pasta, béchamel sauce, and a meat-based sauce (called ragù in Italian). The lasagna that Italian children eat may be slightly different from what you might be used to—they expect a slice of lasagna to stand up on the plate and hold its shape. This recipe shows you how to make lasagna the Italian way.

SERVES	PREPARATION TIME	COOKING TIME
4	15 minutes	1½ hours

FOR THE RAGÙ:

1 carrot

—

1 onion

—

1 garlic clove

—

2 tablespoons olive oil

—

12 ounces good-quality ground beef

—

scant ½ cup water

—

2¼ cups bottled strained tomatoes

—

rosemary sprig, sage leaf, or bay leaf (optional)

1 quantity béchamel sauce (see pages 98–101)

—

2 ounces Parmesan cheese

—

about 12 dried lasagna sheets*

*You can make fresh pasta, if you like (see pages 74–77), or you can buy dried lasagna sheets that are ready to use

LASAGNA

STEP 1

To make the ragù, start by finely chopping the carrot and onion using the bridge and claw techniques (see pages 12–13), and crush the garlic with a garlic crusher (see pages 10–11).

STEP 2

Put the oil, carrot, onion, and garlic in a pan, and cook over low heat for about 10 minutes until really soft, stirring every now and then.

STEP 3

Push the vegetables to the side of the pan and add the beef, making sure it covers the base of the pan. Let it cook until it has turned brown (3–4 minutes). Stir everything together and cook for another 3–4 minutes. Stir every now and then to cook the meat and the vegetables evenly.

STEP 4

Add the water and strained tomatoes and simmer gently (the mixture will be very gently bubbling) for 30 minutes. You can also add a sprig of fresh rosemary or sage or a bay leaf to the ragù for extra flavor if you like. Make the béchamel sauce if you haven't already, and grate the Parmesan cheese (see pages 14–15).

STEP 5

Turn on the oven to 350°F. You will need an ovenproof dish about 10 inches × 8 inches big. Spread a little of the ragù over the base of the dish, then spread a little of the béchamel sauce over the top. Each layer of sauce should be quite thin, like a layer of jam on toast. Then rest a layer of pasta sheets over the top. Keep layering the ragù, the béchamel sauce, and then the pasta sheets.

STEP 6

For this size dish, you should have 4 layers of pasta (3 sheets in each layer). Finish the lasagna with a layer of pasta topped with béchamel sauce. Sprinkle a little grated Parmesan over the top of the lasagna.

STEP 7

Put the dish on a baking tray. Using oven mitts, put the tray in the oven and bake for 35 minutes until golden and bubbling. Serve with salad or cooked greens.

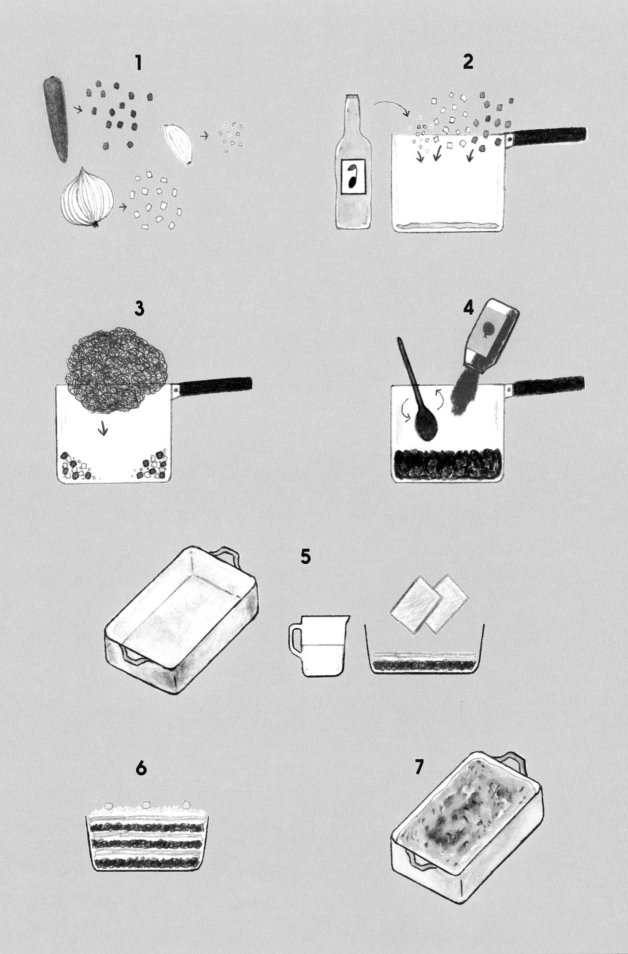

RIGATONI WITH MEATBALLS

Making meatballs is a great way to practice your math and learn about fractions: In this recipe, you have to divide the mixture for the meatballs into eight equal pieces. It's good to make all the meatballs the same size, so that they will cook evenly. Rigatoni is a type of tube-shaped pasta with ridges around the outside, but you could use penne or any other short types of pasta instead.

SERVES	PREPARATION TIME	COOKING TIME
4	30 minutes	1¼ hours

handful of fresh flat-leaf parsley

—

½ garlic clove

—

14 ounces ground beef or
7 ounces each of ground pork
and ground beef

—

freshly ground black pepper

—

1 barnyard egg

—

handful of all-purpose flour,
for dusting

—

1 onion

1 celery stalk

—

1 carrot

—

2 tablespoons olive oil

—

1 small sprig fresh rosemary

—

2¼ cups bottled strained
tomatoes

—

14 ounces dried rigatoni

—

1 ounce Parmesan cheese

RIGATONI WITH MEATBALLS

STEP 1

Using kitchen scissors (see pages 10–11), snip the parsley leaves into small pieces. Crush the garlic (see pages 10–11). Put the ground meat into a large bowl, add the parsley and garlic, and season with some freshly ground black pepper.

STEP 2

Crack the egg into a small bowl (see pages 14–15), and add it to the bowl with the meat.

STEP 3

Put your hands into the bowl with the mixture and mix everything together—you can use a fork if you prefer but it's more fun with your hands.

STEP 4

Divide the meatball mixture in half, then into quarters, and then into eighths.

STEP 5

Using your hands shape the meatball mixture into 8 balls that are all the same size.

STEP 6

Sprinkle the flour onto a plate and then dip each meatball into the flour. Put the meatballs on a plate and into the refrigerator.

STEP 7

Using the bridge and claw cutting techniques (see pages 12–13), chop the onion, celery, and carrot into small pieces.

STEP 8

Put the oil into a heavy pan, add the onion, carrot, and celery, and cook over low heat for 10 minutes, stirring every now and then with a wooden spoon.

STEP 9

Push the carrot mixture to the sides of the pan, add the meatballs, and cook for another 5 minutes without moving the meatballs.

STEP 10

Very carefully turn the meatballs over in the pan so that they brown, making sure they don't fall apart. Add the rosemary and strained tomatoes, and continue to cook gently over low heat for about 40 minutes, until the meatballs are cooked through.

STEP 11

Bring a large pan of water to a boil and cook the rigatoni. (See page 73 for how to cook dried pasta.)

STEP 12

Divide the pasta among your serving bowls, and ladle the meatballs on top. Make sure you throw away the rosemary stalk! Grate the Parmesan (see pages 14–15), and sprinkle over the top.

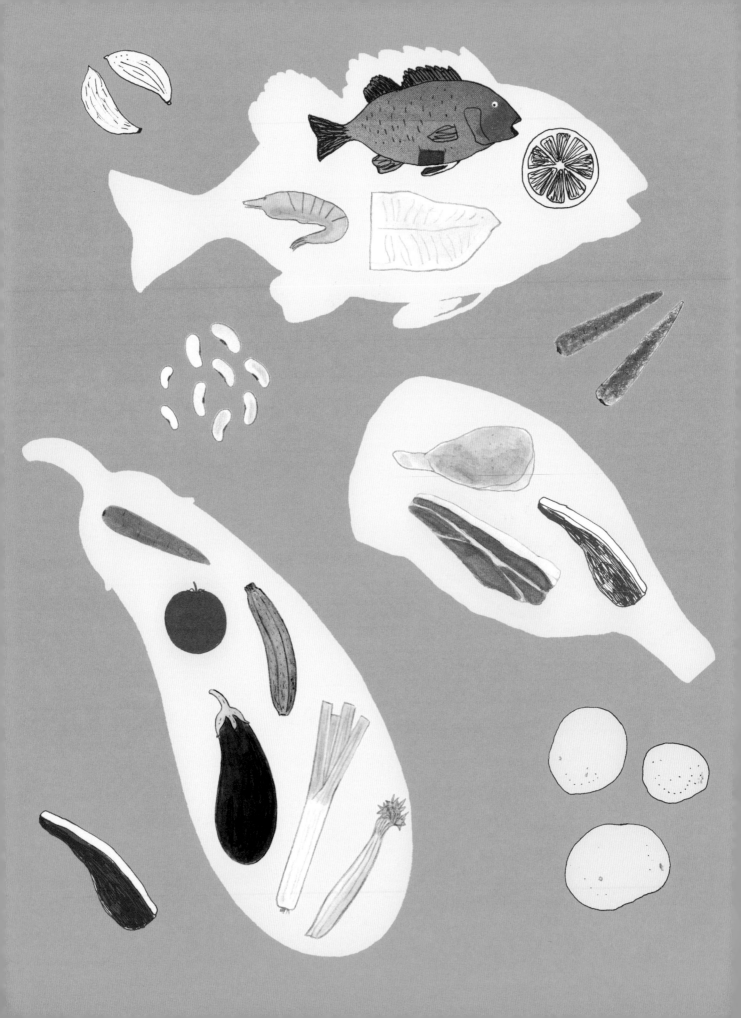

MAIN COURSES

RISOTTO

Risotto is a dish from northern Italy made with rice and stock (a liquid flavored with ingredients such as vegetables or chicken). The most important ingredient is good quality risotto rice, ideally carnaroli or vialone nano, both of which are available from good food shops. When cooked, this rice has a firm texture as well as a creamy softness. This may be hard to imagine, but when you have cooked a good risotto, you'll see what I mean.

Once you know how to make a basic risotto, you can add other ingredients, like vegetables or meat. In Milan, risotto is made with saffron, which adds a beautiful golden color.

SERVES	PREPARATION TIME	COOKING TIME
4	10 minutes	40 minutes

1½ ounces Parmesan cheese

—

5–6¼ cups vegetable or chicken stock
(if you are not using fresh stock, use a good
vegetable bouillon powder)

—

1 onion

—

3 tablespoons sweet butter

—

1 tablespoon olive oil

—

scant 1¾ cups risotto rice

—

½ teaspoon saffron threads

RISOTTO

STEP 1

Carefully grate the Parmesan cheese (see page 14–15), and put to one side. Pour the stock into a pan and bring up to simmering point—this is when it is very gently bubbling. Get a ladle and put it by the pan, ready for later.

STEP 2

Using the bridge and claw cutting techniques (see pages 12–13), chop the onion. Melt half the butter and oil in a heavy pan (the butter adds flavor and the oil keeps it from burning). Add the onion and cook gently for 10 minutes until it is really soft, stirring occasionally with a wooden spoon. This stage is known in Italy as the "soffritto," and it forms the base of the risotto. If you are making a different flavored risotto, you would add your other ingredients, such as garlic or mushrooms or sausage meat, at this stage.

STEP 3

The next stage is known as the "tostatura," or the toasting of the rice. Add the rice to the pan and stir to coat it thoroughly with the onion and butter.

STEP 4

Carefully add a couple of ladles of hot stock and the saffron threads, and stir gently until all the liquid has been absorbed by the rice. Then add another couple of ladles of hot stock and cook, still stirring, until it has been absorbed.

STEP 5

Keep adding the stock in this way until it has all been used up—only add more stock when the liquid in the pan has been absorbed. It should take about 18–20 minutes until the rice is cooked and all the stock has been absorbed.

Take a small spoon and taste the rice to see if it is ready—it should be soft but still have some "bite," and it will also taste slightly creamy.

STEP 6

Lower the heat and add the remaining butter and the grated Parmesan cheese, and stir—this stage is called the "mantecatura," and it helps to give the risotto its lovely texture. Serve immediately.

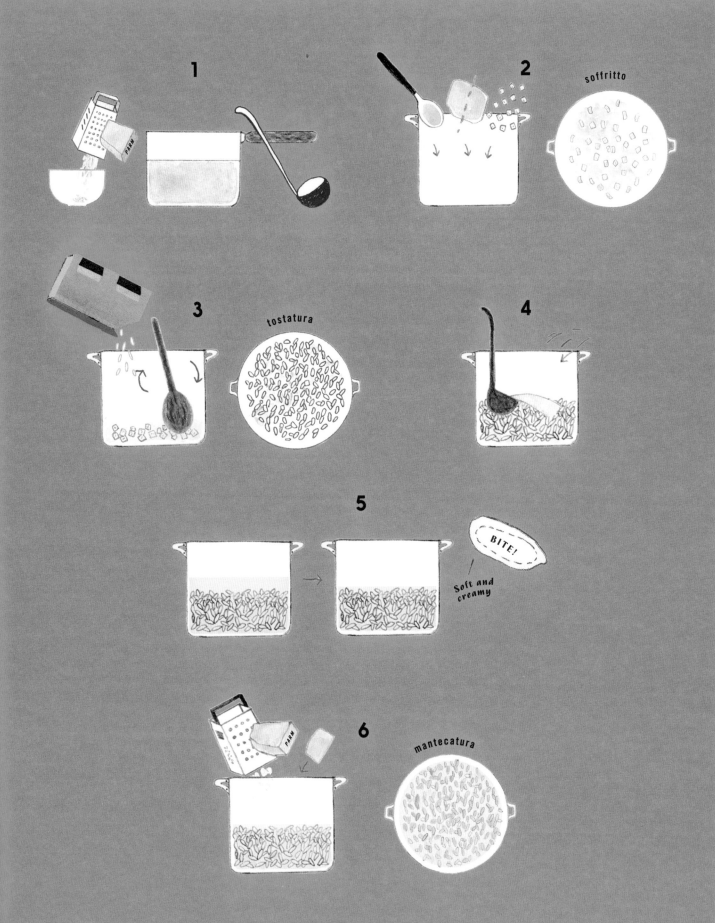

1

2

soffritto

3

tostatura

4

5

BITE!

Soft and
creamy

6

mantecatura

POTATO GNOCCHI

Gnocchi (pronounced "nee-ockee") are little dumplings that can be made from potatoes, flour, or cornmeal. Many regions of Italy have their own special types of gnocchi. They are easy to make and great fun to shape! Gnocchi can be eaten with different sauces, like tomato sauce (see pages 86–89) or pesto (see pages 94–97).

SERVES	PREPARATION TIME	COOKING TIME
4	30 minutes	30 minutes

2¼ pounds potatoes

—

1 extra-large barnyard egg

—

scant 2¼ cups all-purpose flour

POTATO GNOCCHI

STEP 1

Using a vegetable peeler, peel the potatoes (see pages 14–15).

STEP 2

Using the bridge technique (see pages 12–13) cut each potato in half. Then rest the halves cut side down on a cutting board and cut them into quarters. Put the potatoes into a colander.

STEP 3

Half-fill a pan with water and put the colander on top. Cover with a lid, bring up to a boil, and then steam the potatoes for 20 minutes. Cooked like this, the potatoes don't absorb too much water—you want them to be quite dry to make the gnocchi.

STEP 4

Turn off the heat. Ask an adult to help you take the colander off the pan. Carefully poke a skewer or fork into a potato to see if it is cooked—the skewer should glide easily into the potato.

STEP 5

Put the potatoes into a bowl and using a potato masher, or a potato ricer, mash until smooth. A potato ricer looks like a very big garlic crusher, and works in the same way. Let cool.

STEP 6

Crack the egg into a bowl (see pages 14–15). Add the flour and egg to the cooled mashed potato and mix with a wooden spoon. Then put your hands into the bowl and mix to make a dough.

STEP 7

Sprinkle some flour over your work counter. Shape the dough into a square about ½ inch thick. Using a table knife, cut the square in half. Cut each half into thin strips about ½ inch wide.

STEP 8

Roll each strip into a long thin sausage with your hands. Cut each sausage into small pieces about ½ inch long, so you have lots of small cylindrical pieces. It doesn't matter if the pieces of dough are slightly different shapes, but you do want them to be even in size so that they take the same amount of time to cook.

STEP 9

Gnocchi traditionally has a pattern on it. Do this by pushing the gnocchi against a grater or a fork. Sprinkle some flour over a big plate or baking sheet, and put the gnocchi on the flour.

STEP 10

Heat a serving dish in a low oven to keep your gnocchi warm when cooked. Bring a large pan of water to a boil, add 8 pieces of gnocchi, and wait for them to rise to the surface. They are cooked when they come up to the top—this will only take about 1 minute.

STEP 11

Using a slotted spoon transfer the gnocchi to the warm serving dish. Cook the rest. Ladle the sauce on top, and it's ready to eat!

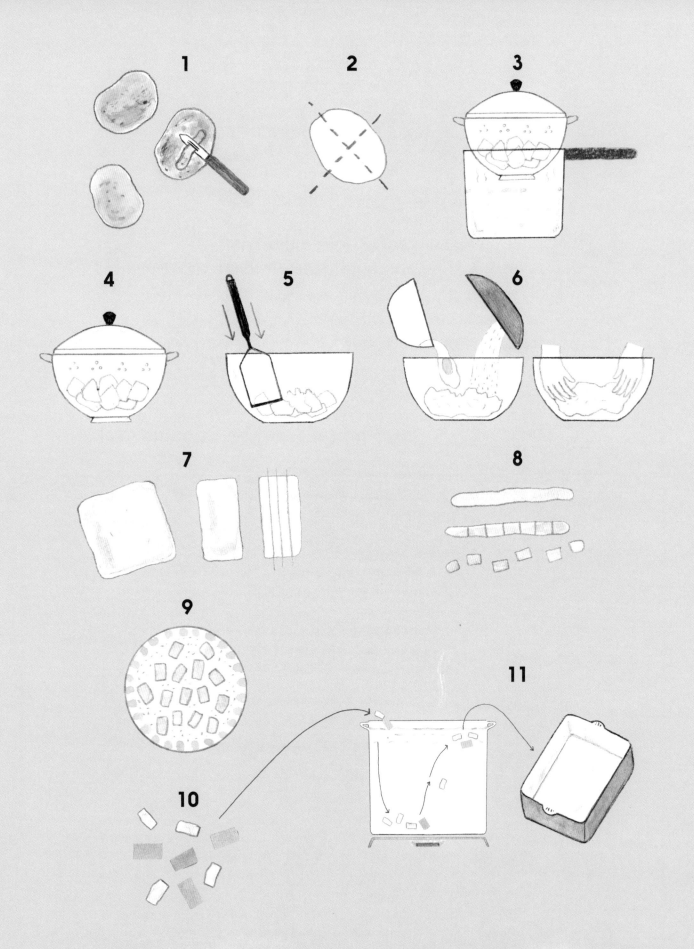

POLENTA GNOCCHI

Polenta is a type of coarse flour made from corn. It looks
like a thick yellow porridge while it's cooking. It needs
a lot of stirring, but then it sets into a solid slab that
you can cut out into different shapes. It's delicious
served with melted butter and cheese, which is how
the Italians often eat it.

SERVES	PREPARATION TIME	COOKING TIME
4	10 minutes	30 minutes

a little olive oil for brushing the tray

—

scant 2½ cups coarse polenta flour

—

1½ ounces Parmesan cheese

—

1½ tablespoons sweet butter

POLENTA GNOCCHI

STEP 1
You will need a baking tray that is about 8 inches × 12 inches big. Brush a little olive oil over your baking tray.

STEP 2
Check the directions on your packet of polenta. Most polenta flours are similar, but it is always worth checking! You will need to measure out the water as directed on the packet, pour it into a big pan, and bring it to a boil.

STEP 3
Very carefully pour the polenta flour into the water—you may need to ask an adult to help you do this. You will need to stir the polenta flour in the water with a wooden spoon to make sure that it doesn't go lumpy.

STEP 4
Lower the heat and cook gently, and keep stirring all the time until the polenta is thick and smooth. This will take about 3 minutes, or the length of time suggested on the packet.

STEP 5
Carefully spoon the polenta mixture onto the baking tray. You might like to use a ladle to do this. Spread out the polenta to make an even rectangle and let cool and set.

STEP 6
When the polenta is cold, stamp out the rounds using a glass—dip the edge of the glass in water to stop the polenta from sticking to it. You could also use a cookie cutter (about 2½ inches in diameter). Start cutting the rounds along one edge of the polenta to make sure that you can cut out as many as possible.

STEP 7
Turn on the oven to 350° F. Brush a little oil over a wide cookie sheet. Arrange a circle of the polenta rounds on the sheet. Top with another smaller layer of polenta rounds and keep layering the rounds until you have a flat pyramid shape. You could make one big pyramid or two small ones.

STEP 8
Carefully grate the Parmesan (see pages 14–15), making sure that your fingers stay well away from the grater. Sprinkle the Parmesan over the polenta stacks and dot with butter. Wearing your oven mitts, put in the oven and bake for 20 minutes until golden brown. Serve with cooked greens of your choice, like beans or broccoli.

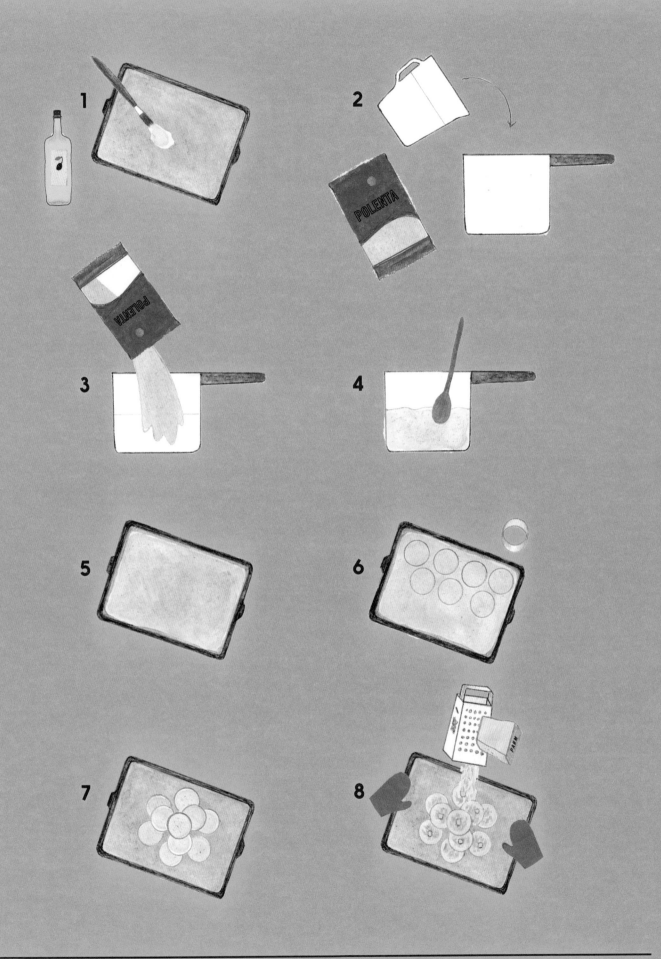

BAKED EGGPLANT WITH TOMATO

Eggplants have beautiful purple shiny skins, and they are delicious cooked in this way with tomatoes and cheese. This recipe is fantastic on its own with bread and salad, or served alongside a main course such as roast chicken or lamb.

SERVES	PREPARATION TIME	COOKING TIME
4	25 minutes	1 hour

2 eggplants

—

3 tablespoons olive oil

—

2 onions

—

2 garlic cloves

—

14-ounce can chopped tomatoes

—

1 fresh flat-leaf parsley sprig

—

3 ounces Emmenthal cheese

—

1 cup bread crumbs

—

a small piece of sweet butter

BAKED EGGPLANT WITH TOMATO

STEP 1

Turn on the oven to 400°F. Using the claw cutting technique (see pages 12–13), slice the eggplants into rounds. Make the slices about ¼ inch thick if you can—they can be a bit thicker if you find that easier.

STEP 2

Brush a roasting dish with a tablespoon of olive oil and arrange the eggplant slices over the dish in one single layer, so that they are not overlapping each other.

Brush the slices with another tablespoon of oil. Wearing your oven mitts, put the tray into the oven and roast for 20 minutes until soft and slightly golden.

STEP 3

Meanwhile, using the bridge and claw cutting techniques (see pages 12–13), chop the onions. Crush the garlic using a garlic crusher (see pages 10–11). Put the rest of the olive oil in a pan, add the onion and garlic, and cook gently over low heat for 5 minutes, stirring every now and then with a wooden spoon.

STEP 4

Add the chopped tomatoes to the pan. Using kitchen scissors (see pages 10–11), snip the parsley into small pieces and add to the pan. Simmer gently for about 15 minutes until the sauce has thickened.

STEP 5

Arrange a layer of eggplant slices in the bottom of an ovenproof dish, ladle or spoon half the tomato sauce over the top, cover with another layer of eggplant slices, and then top with another layer of tomato sauce.

STEP 6

Grate the cheese carefully into a small bowl, making sure that your fingers stay well away from the grater (see pages 14–15). Add the bread crumbs, mix together, and sprinkle over the top of the eggplant.

STEP 7

Put the ovenproof dish onto a baking tray and dot with butter. Wearing your oven mitts, put the tray in the oven and bake for 20 minutes until golden. Serve hot.

1

2

3

4

5

6

7

BEANS WITH SAUSAGES

Beans and sausages are a classic combination, simple and delicious. In this recipe, you pour some apple juice in with the beans, which may sound a bit strange at first, but it makes for a really wonderful sweet sauce for the beans!

SERVES	PREPARATION TIME	COOKING TIME
4	5 minutes	40 minutes

8–12 good quality pork sausages
(depending on how many you want to eat!)

—

2 garlic cloves

—

2 teaspoons olive oil

—

2 fresh sage leaves

—

14-ounce can cannellini beans, rinsed and drained

—

scant ½ cup apple juice

—

freshly ground black pepper

BEANS WITH SAUSAGES

STEP 1

Turn on the oven to 375°F. Prick the sausages all over with a fork. Put into a heavy roasting dish, add the whole garlic cloves with the skin left on and the olive oil. Using oven mitts, put into the oven for 20 minutes. The sausages will turn lovely and brown as they cook in the roasting dish—this will help color the beans and the gravy juice later.

STEP 2

Put your oven mitts on and take the roasting dish out of the oven. Using tongs or a knife and fork, carefully turn the sausages over. The sausages will then go brown on the other side when they go back in the oven.

STEP 3

Very carefully spoon out any spare fat that has collected in the bottom of the dish. Coarsely tear the sage and add to the sausages with the canned beans. Add the apple juice and stir.

STEP 4

Wearing your oven mitts, put back into the oven for another 20 minutes until the beans are hot and slightly soft. Carefully stir everything with a wooden spoon, and add a little freshly ground black pepper. Serve with some fresh cooked greens. If you like, you can serve the beans and sausages in a pretty dish, but it's not necessary!

BAKED COD WITH VEGETABLES

This dish looks good and tastes great, with the colorful vegetables sitting under the white cod wrapped in the pink pancetta. Any firm white fish, such as hake, gurnard, or haddock, will be equally delicious in this recipe.

SERVES	PREPARATION TIME	COOKING TIME
4	20 minutes	40 minutes

1 small leek or ½ big leek

—

2 carrots

—

7-ounce can chopped tomatoes

—

1½ tablespoons sweet butter

—

1 tablespoon olive oil

—

4 cod fillets, or any other firm white fish, skin removed

—

1 lemon

—

8 slices pancetta

BAKED COD WITH VEGETABLES

STEP 1

Turn on the oven to 375°F. Wash the leek and, using the bridge cutting technique (see pages 12–13), trim off the roots and dark green leaves. Using the claw technique (see pages 12–13), cut the leek into slices, as thinly as possible.

STEP 2

Wash and peel the carrots. Using the bridge technique again, trim the tips off the top and bottom of the carrot, then slice it in half widthwise, and then in half lengthwise. Rest the flat sides of the carrot on a board and cut into thin slices using the claw technique.

STEP 3

Put the tomatoes, leek, and carrots into a heavy roasting pan, dot with the butter, and drizzle with the oil. Wearing your oven mitts, put the pan in the oven and roast for 20 minutes.

STEP 4

While the vegetables are cooking, put the fish fillets onto a cutting board and check for any bones. Carefully run your fingers over the pieces of fish and if you feel a bone, pull it out with tweezers.

STEP 5

Using the bridge technique, cut the lemon in half. Squeeze the lemon juice over the fish, and brush any lemon seeds to the side so you can throw them away.

STEP 6

Put 2 slices of pancetta onto the board, put a cod fillet onto the pancetta, and then wrap the pancetta around the fish. Repeat with the other fillets.

STEP 7

When the vegetables have cooked for 20 minutes, using your oven mitts, take the roasting pan out of the oven. Carefully put the fish on top of the vegetables, with the pancetta "seam" facing downward. Using your oven mitts, put the roasting pan back in the oven and cook for another 10–15 minutes. Then cut one of the fillets in half to check that it is cooked: The fish should be white and opaque instead of slightly transparent. If it is not cooked all the way through, cook for another 5 minutes.

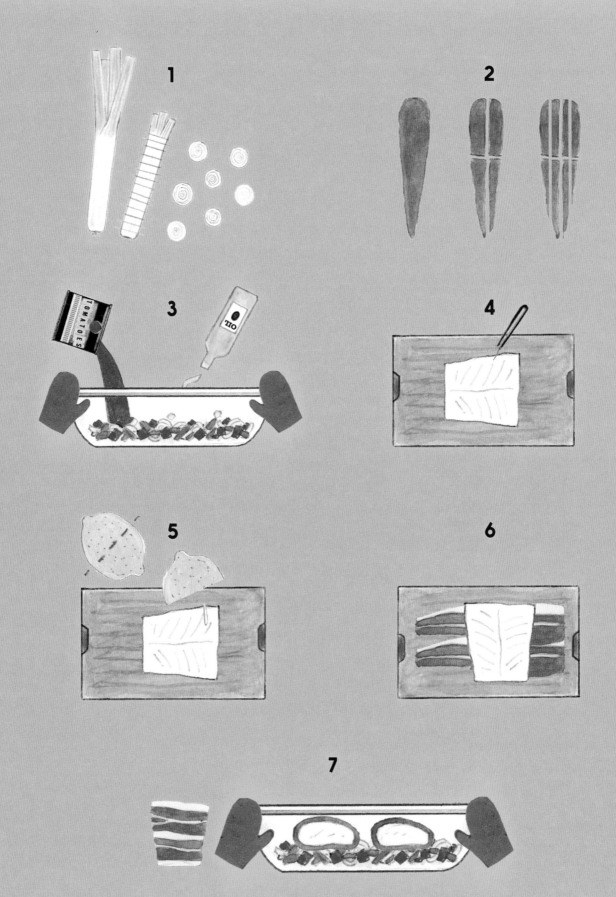

FISH KABOBS

This recipe calls for a variety of different types of fish, so ask for a selection of fresh fish for fish kabobs at the grocery store. You'll notice when you buy them that some types of raw shrimp are grey—they only turn pink when they are cooked! If you buy shrimp with their shells, you'll need to peel them before making the kabobs. These kabobs are also great cooked on a barbecue.

MAKES	PREPARATION TIME	COOKING TIME
8 kabobs	35 minutes	15 minutes

You will need 8 wooden skewers

1¾ pounds fresh fish, for example tilapia, gurnard, whiting, pollack, salmon, haddock, and cod

—

8 big raw shrimps, peeled

—

handful of small mushrooms

—

handful of cherry tomatoes

—

handful of pitted olives

—

lemon wedges, to serve

FOR THE MARINADE:

1 garlic clove

—

½ lemon

—

2 tablespoons olive oil

—

small handful fresh flat-leaf parsley leaves

THE SILVER SPOON FOR CHILDREN | 137

FISH KABOBS

STEP 1

Turn on the oven to 375°F. Put the pieces of fish onto a cutting board, remove any skin, and run your fingers over them checking for bones. Use tweezers to pull out any bones you find.

STEP 2

Using the bridge technique (see pages 12–13), cut the fish into big chunks—about 1 inch square. If you cut the fish too small, it is more likely to fall off the skewers.

STEP 3

To make the marinade, peel and crush the garlic and put into a bowl. Squeeze the lemon juice onto the garlic. Add the oil and mix together. Using kitchen scissors, snip the parsley leaves and add to the oil mixture. Mix everything together with a spoon. (See pages 11–15 to remind yourself how to do these things!)

STEP 4

Hold a piece of fish between your thumb and finger and push a skewer though the middle of the fish. Carry on pushing pieces of fish onto the skewer, alternating the different types of fish with shrimp, mushrooms, tomatoes, and olives. You can make up your own special sequence, so that you know which one is yours when the kabobs come out of the oven!

STEP 5

Put the kabobs into a large ovenproof dish, pour the marinade over the fish and carefully move the kabobs around to make sure that they are covered with the marinade. Let marinate in the refrigerator for about 20 minutes.

STEP 6

Put your oven mitts on, put the fish into the oven, and cook for 10 minutes. Take the dish out of the oven and, using oven mitts or tongs, turn the skewers over. Wearing your oven mitts, put back into the oven and cook for another 5 minutes or until cooked through. Serve hot.

CHICKEN STEW WITH OLIVES

Olives are green or black. They grow on trees, and the green olives are picked quite early, when they are still young. The black ones are picked later, when they are riper. They are often softer and have a milder flavor. You can use any pieces of chicken you like for this recipe, such as thighs or legs. Serve this stew with polenta, bread, pasta, rice, or potatoes. This is a tasty, simple dish—with just a few basic ingredients, you can make a classic Italian meal!

SERVES	PREPARATION TIME	COOKING TIME
4	15 minutes	50 minutes

4 large pieces or 8 small pieces of chicken, such as legs or thighs

—

1 tablespoon sweet butter

—

1 tablespoon olive oil

—

1¼ cups black olives

—

14-ounce can chopped tomatoes

—

1 teaspoon light brown soft sugar

—

4 fresh basil leaves

—

1 fresh parsley sprig

CHICKEN STEW WITH OLIVES

STEP 1	Turn on the oven to 325°F. Pull the skin away from the pieces of chicken. Put the butter and oil in a heavy flameproof casserole dish, heat on the stove until the butter has melted, add the chicken pieces, and cook over medium heat for 5 minutes without touching the chicken.
STEP 2	Using tongs, turn the chicken pieces over—they should be a nice golden color on one side. Cook for another 3 minutes. Take off the heat.
STEP 3	Using a rolling pin, carefully squash an olive slightly so you can open it up and take the pit out. Do this with all the olives.
STEP 4	Pour the canned tomatoes over the chicken, fill the empty can with water, and add to the chicken with the olives and sugar. Stir with a wooden spoon, cover with a lid, and, using oven mitts, put in the oven, and cook for 40 minutes.
STEP 5	Wearing your oven mitts, take the casserole dish out of the oven. Tear the basil and use kitchen scissors (see pages 10–11) to snip the parsley. Sprinkle the herbs over the top and serve with polenta, bread, pasta, rice, or potatoes.

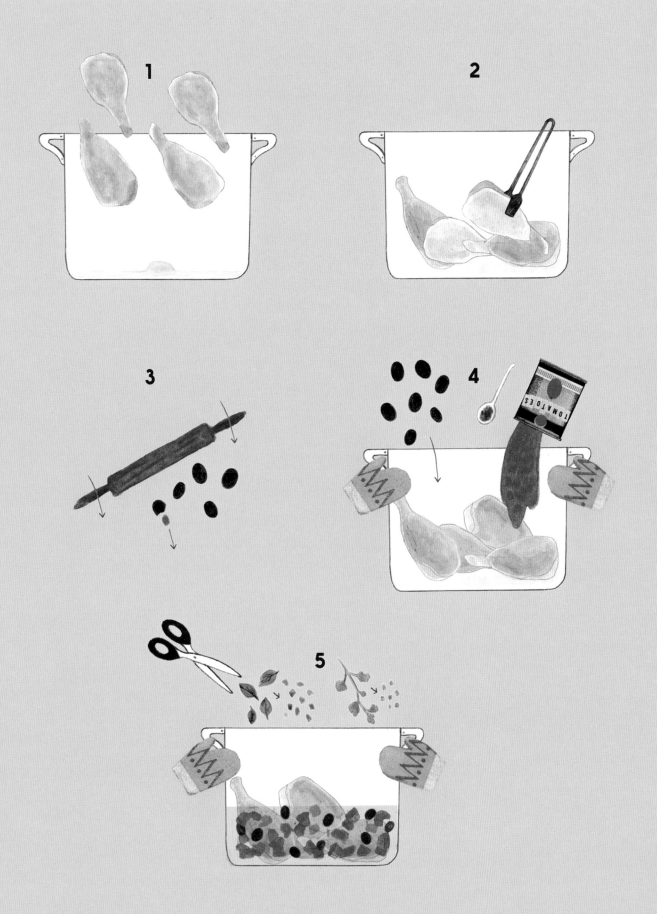

CHICKEN FILLETS STUFFED WITH MASCARPONE

Mascarpone is a rich creamy cheese, which can be used in both savory and sweet dishes. Serve these stuffed chicken fillets with fresh steamed vegetables, like broccoli or green beans, and potatoes or rice.

SERVES	PREPARATION TIME	COOKING TIME
4	30 minutes	30 minutes

4 ounces mushrooms (any type will do)

—

1 garlic clove

—

handful fresh flat-leaf parsley leaves

—

1 teaspoon olive oil

—

1½ tablespoons sweet butter

—

4 skinless, boneless chicken fillet portions

—

scant ½ cup mascarpone cheese

—

4 slices prosciutto (see page 18)

—

freshly ground black pepper

CHICKEN FILLETS STUFFED WITH MASCARPONE

STEP 1

Turn on the oven to 400°F. Using the bridge and claw cutting techniques (see pages 12–13), chop the mushrooms in half and then slice them as thinly as possible.

STEP 2

Peel the papery skin away from the garlic clove and crush the garlic with a garlic crusher. Snip the parsley leaves with kitchen scissors (see pages 10–11).

STEP 3

Put the oil and butter into a small pan, add the garlic, mushrooms, and parsley, and cook over low heat for 5 minutes until the mushrooms are soft.

STEP 4

Add a little freshly ground black pepper. Spoon the mushrooms into a bowl and leave until the mixture is really cool. This is important, as you don't want to put hot mixture in the uncooked chicken fillets.

STEP 5

Ask an adult to help you cut a slit in the chicken. Put a piece of chicken on a cutting board. Holding your hand flat on top of the chicken fillet, very carefully slice into the side of the chicken without cutting all the way through, then open the piece of chicken like a book. Cover the chicken with a piece of plastic wrap. Using a rolling pin, carefully bash the chicken fillet—you want to flatten it slightly so that it cooks quickly in the oven and stays moist. Do the same with the other pieces of chicken. Don't forget to wash the rolling pin carefully after you have used it to flatten the chicken!

STEP 6

Add the mascarpone to the cooled mushrooms and mix together.

STEP 7

Divide the mushroom mixture among the middle of the chicken fillets and then close the flap over the mixture. Wrap a slice of prosciutto around the chicken and put the chicken wrapped in ham onto a roasting pan, with the "seam" facing downward.

STEP 8

Wearing your oven mitts, put the tray into the oven and roast for 20 minutes. Cut one chicken fillet in half to check that it is cooked all the way through. If it is at all pink, put it back in the oven for another 5 minutes or until it's well cooked.

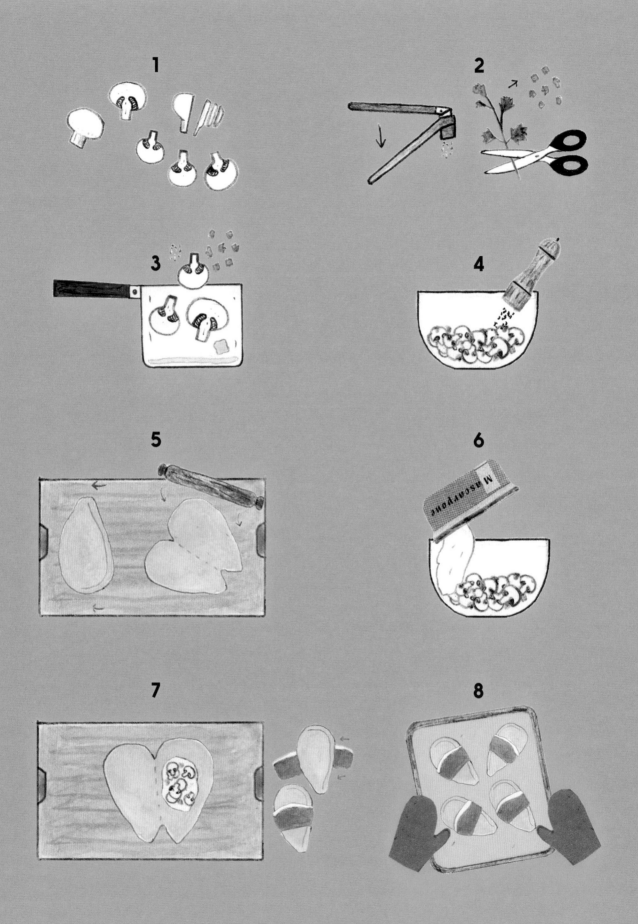

BEEF STEW

It's really useful to learn how to make a stew. Not only does it taste great, it's all cooked in one pan, so there's not much to wash! And once it's in the oven, you can go off and do something else while it cooks. Serve this stew with mashed potatoes or new potatoes with rosemary (see pages 152–155).

SERVES	PREPARATION TIME	COOKING TIME
4	15 minutes	2¼ hours

5 ounces pancetta or bacon bits

—

1 onion

—

1 celery stalk

—

1 carrot

—

1 tablespoon olive oil

—

1 pound 5 ounces lean stewing steak (ask your butcher to cut the beef into small chunks)

—

14-ounce can chopped tomatoes

—

1 teaspoon light brown soft sugar

—

1 rosemary sprig

—

1¾ cups vegetable stock (if you are not using fresh stock, use a good vegetable bouillon powder)

—

freshly ground black pepper

BEEF STEW

STEP 1

Turn on the oven to 300°F. If your pancetta or bacon is not already cubed, use the bridge technique (see pages 12–13) to cut the slices into small pieces—first into thin strips and then into small cubes.

STEP 2

Using the bridge and claw cutting techniques (see pages 12–13), chop the onion, celery, and carrot into small pieces.

STEP 3

Put the oil in a heavy flameproof casserole dish and add the pancetta, onion, celery, and carrot, and cook gently over low heat for 10 minutes. Stir occasionally with a wooden spoon.

STEP 4

Push the vegetables to the sides of the pan, add the meat and cook until just brown—this will take about 5 minutes. If you prefer, you can spoon the vegetables out of the pan onto a plate so you can cook the meat in the empty pan, and then put the vegetables back afterward.

STEP 5

Add the tomatoes, sugar, and rosemary. Fill the empty tomato can with stock and add to the pan—this helps to make sure that you use all the tomato juices in the can. Add any leftover stock to the pan.

STEP 6

Stir everything together with a wooden spoon. Wearing your oven mitts, put the pan into the oven and cook very gently for 2 hours. You might need to ask an adult to check if the oven temperature needs to be lowered. Season with freshly ground black pepper before serving.

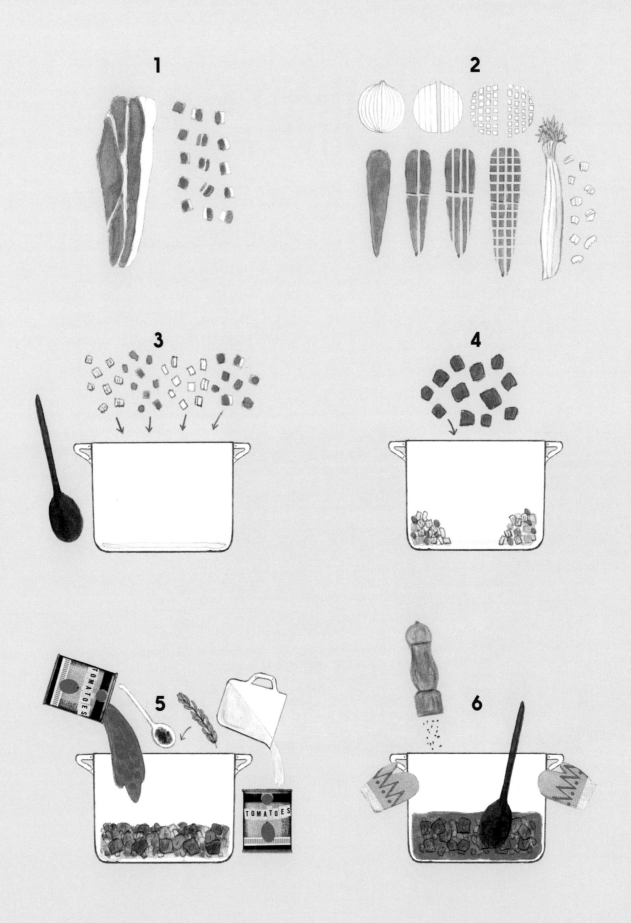

LAMB CHOPS & NEW POTATOES WITH ROSEMARY

Lamb is really tasty when it's cooked with fresh herbs such as mint. In Italy, it is almost always cooked with herbs. This recipe uses a marinade—this mixture of lemon juice, oil, and herbs helps to make the lamb more tender and flavorsome.

SERVES	PREPARATION TIME	COOKING TIME
4	1¼ hours	40 minutes

1 lemon

—

1 fresh mint sprig

—

2 tablespoons olive oil

—

4 lamb chops

FOR THE ROASTED NEW POTATOES:

1½ pounds new potatoes

—

1 fresh rosemary sprig

—

1 garlic clove

—

2 tablespoons olive oil

LAMB CHOPS & NEW POTATOES WITH ROSEMARY

STEP 1

Using the bridge technique (see pages 12–13), cut the lemon in half and then squeeze its juice into a bowl (see pages 14–15). Pull the mint leaves off the stalk and add to the lemon juice with the oil, and mix everything together.

STEP 2

Put the lamb chops into the lemon juice mixture and mix to make sure that the meat is well coated in the oil.

STEP 3

Let marinate for 1 hour. This gives the lamb chops time to absorb all those lovely oil and herb flavors—you will find that the lamb is really tender and has wonderful flavor when it is cooked.

STEP 4

Once the lamb has been marinating for 45 minutes, turn on the oven to 375°F. Using the bridge technique, cut the potatoes in half lengthwise and put into a roasting pan with the rosemary and garlic. Drizzle over the oil and, using oven mitts, put the pan in the oven and roast for 20 minutes.

STEP 5

Take the lamb out of the marinade and if your pan is big enough, add the lamb to the potatoes. If not, you will need another roasting dish for the lamb. Roast the lamb chops for 10 minutes. Wearing your oven mitts, take the lamb out of the oven and, using tongs, turn the chops over.

STEP 6

Using oven mitts, put the dish back into the oven for another 10 minutes. The potatoes should be golden and tender when you poke them with a skewer or table knife. The lamb will be very slightly pink in the middle, which is how it should be. Cook for a little bit longer if you prefer.

ROAST LEG OF LAMB IN A HERB CRUST WITH STUFFED TOMATOES

This is a great dish for a big family dinner or celebration. It goes really well with the stuffed tomatoes included in this recipe, but you could also eat it with broccoli or green beans. You can try other herb combinations: Fresh mint instead of thyme also tastes good. The cooking times given in this recipe will mean that the lamb is slightly pink in the middle, so cook it for 10 minutes longer if you prefer.

SERVES	PREPARATION TIME	COOKING TIME
6	15 minutes	1 hour 20 minutes

1 fresh thyme or mint sprig

—

1 fresh oregano sprig or
2 teaspoons dried oregano

—

1 fresh flat-leaf parsley sprig

—

1 fresh rosemary sprig

—

1 slice toasted bread,
white or brown

—

2 tablespoons olive oil

—

3-pound leg of lamb

FOR THE STUFFED TOMATOES:

4 ripe tomatoes

—

2 slices toasted bread,
white or brown

—

a few fresh oregano leaves

—

1 tablespoon olive oil

ROAST LEG OF LAMB IN A HERB CRUST WITH STUFFED TOMATOES

STEP 1

Turn on the oven to 400°F. Pull the herb leaves off the stalks, then using kitchen scissors (see pages 10–11), snip the leaves into small pieces and put into a bowl together.

STEP 2

Crumble the piece of toast into bread crumbs using your fingers. Add to the bowl of herbs.

STEP 3

Add the oil to the herbs and bread crumbs, and mix well.

STEP 4

Put the leg of lamb into a big roasting pan and use your hands to spread the herb mixture all over the meat. Add ⅔ cup water to the roasting pan. Using oven mitts, put the pan into the oven and roast for 15 minutes.

STEP 5

Lower the oven temperature to 350°F and roast for another 35 minutes. These timings are correct for a 3-pound leg of lamb, so if yours is a different weight, you will need to put some math to good use! You will need to cook the lamb for 20 minutes per pound, plus another 20 minutes. Or to put it another way, for about 4 minutes for every 3 ounces of lamb plus 20 minutes.

STEP 6

In the meantime, cut the tomatoes in half using the bridge technique (see pages 12–13). Scoop out the seeds with a teaspoon.

STEP 7

Crumble the other 2 pieces of toast with your fingers and spoon into the tomatoes. Sprinkle over the oregano and drizzle over the oil.

STEP 8

When the lamb has been in the oven for 35 minutes, ask an adult to help you take the roasting pan out of the oven. Add the tomatoes to the pan and put back in the oven. Or you can put the tomatoes into an ovenproof dish and using oven mitts, put it into the oven next to the roasting pan. Roast the tomatoes and lamb for another 25 minutes. Using your oven mitts, take the lamb out of the oven and let rest for 5 minutes before serving.

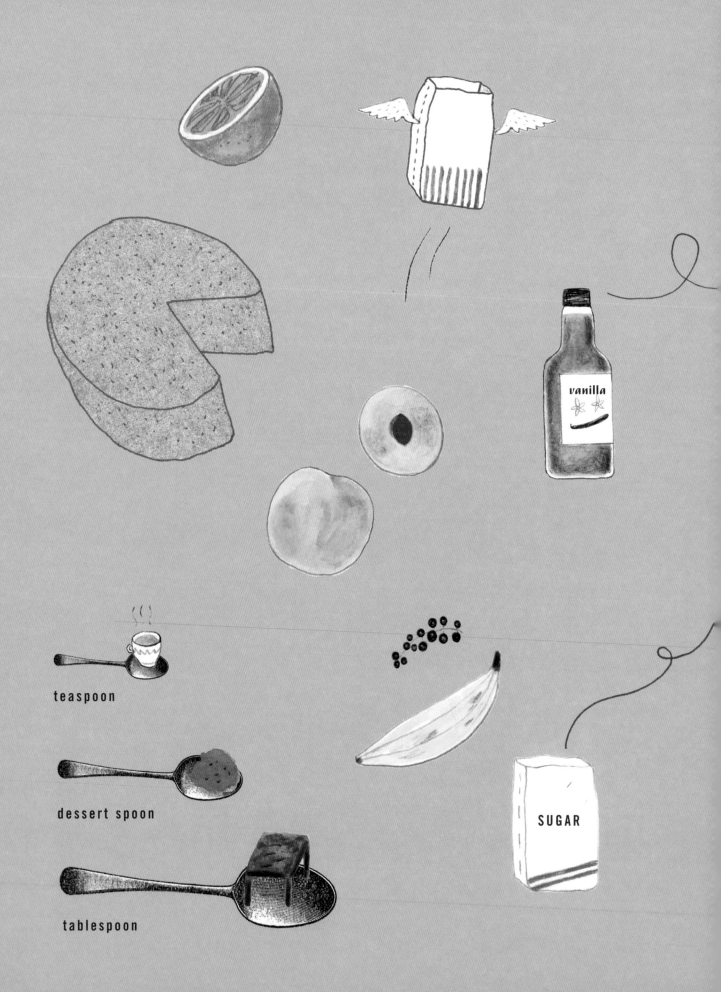

teaspoon

dessert spoon

tablespoon

vanilla

SUGAR

BAKING & DESSERTS

FOCACCIA

Focaccia is a type of flat bread that is really popular in Italy. It has dimples all over to hold the delicious flavors of olive oil and rosemary, and is very easy to make. Once you've made this version, you could try adding other flavors on top, such as grated cheese, sun-dried tomatoes, or olives.

MAKES	PREPARATION TIME	COOKING TIME
1 big loaf	1¼ hours	25 minutes

3–4 tablespoons olive oil, plus extra for brushing the tray

—

4½ cups strong bread flour, plus extra for dusting

—

1 envelope (⅛ ounce) active dry yeast

FOR THE TOPPING:

2 tablespoons olive oil

—

a handful fresh rosemary leaves,
or another topping of your choice

FOCACCIA

STEP 1

Start by pouring ½ cup cold water into your measuring cup and then add enough hot water to make 1 cup. Dip your finger in to test the temperature—it should feel just warm.

STEP 2

Using a pastry brush, brush an 8 inch × 12 inch baking sheet with a little olive oil, then sprinkle a little flour over the tray.

STEP 3

Sift the flour into a really big bowl. Sprinkle the dry yeast over the flour.

STEP 4

Make a well—a big hole—in the middle of the flour (you should be able to see the bottom of the bowl).

STEP 5

Mix the oil with the water in a pitcher and pour the warm water into the well. Use a wooden spoon to mix to a soft dough.

STEP 6

Sprinkle a little flour over the counter and put the dough onto the flour. Knead the dough by pushing it away from you with the base of your hands and then pulling it back with your fingers. Do this for about 5 minutes until you can stretch the dough like a big piece of elastic. Using your hands and a rolling pin, stretch it into a rectangular shape, just a bit smaller than your baking sheet, and put the dough into the tray. Cover with a slightly damp dish towel and leave in a warm place for about 1 hour, until it has doubled in size—watch it grow!

STEP 7

Turn on the oven to 425°F. Push your thumb into the dough all over to make dimples. Drizzle the oil over the top and sprinkle with the rosemary. Using oven mitts, put the baking sheet into the oven and bake for 20–25 minutes until golden and cooked. Cut into rectangles, or tear it into pieces and share.

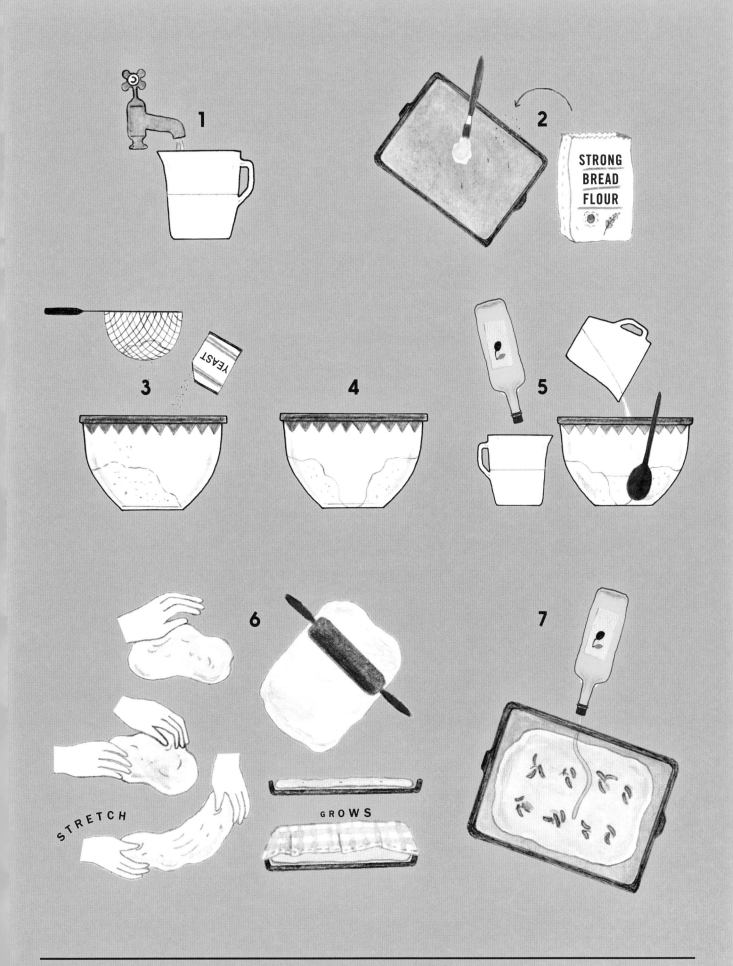

1

2

STRONG
BREAD
FLOUR

3

YEAST

4

5

6

STRETCH

GROWS

7

MARBLE RING CAKE

This chocolate and vanilla cake is quite firm and not too sweet. It's great served for dessert with fruit, or you could pack a slice to take to school as a snack. You could even try toasting and buttering a slice—it's delicious!

SERVES	PREPARATION TIME	COOKING TIME
6—8	20 minutes	25 minutes

7 tablespoons sweet butter, plus a little extra
for greasing the cake pan

—

3½ cups self-rising flour

—

2 barnyard eggs

—

¾ cup milk plus 1 tablespoon milk

—

a few drops vanilla extract

—

1 teaspoon baking powder

—

½ cup superfine sugar

—

2 tablespoons unsweetened cocoa powder

—

unsweetened cocoa powder or
confectioner's sugar to decorate

MARBLE RING CAKE

STEP 1

Turn on the oven to 350°F. Grease a 9-inch ring mold (or you could use an 8-inch round cake pan)—rub a little butter all over the inside. Sprinkle a little flour over the mold.

STEP 2

Put the butter into a small pan and melt over gentle heat or melt in a small bowl in the microwave. Let cool.

STEP 3

Crack the eggs into a small bowl (see pages 14–15). Add the cooled melted butter, milk, and vanilla extract to the eggs, and whisk together with a fork.

STEP 4

Sift the flour and baking powder into a big bowl. Add the sugar.

STEP 5

Pour the egg mixture into the bowl with the flour and carefully stir everything together.

STEP 6

Spoon half of the mixture into another bowl, add the cocoa powder and 1 tablespoon of milk, and mix again.

STEP 7

Spoon the chocolate mixture into the greased mold. The cake mixture is quite stiff, so you will need to use two spoons to spoon it into the pan. Make sure it goes all the way around the pan!

STEP 8

Spoon the vanilla cake mixture on top of the chocolate mixture. Whichever cake mixture you put into the pan first will come out on the top of the cake. If you want to create a really "marbled" cake, you can spoon alternate spoonfuls of each mixture into the pan, so that the finished cake has a swirly pattern instead of a layer of vanilla with a layer of chocolate on top of it.

STEP 9

Using oven mitts, put the cake in the oven and bake for 20 minutes. To see if it is cooked, poke a skewer or knife into the cake—it should come out clean. If there is any sticky cake mixture on the skewer, put the cake back into the oven for 3–4 minutes. Put the cake pan on a cooling rack and leave for about 15 minutes. Carefully turn the cake pan upside down and take the cake out of the pan. Let cool.

STEP 10

Using a small strainer, sprinkle unsweetened cocoa powder or confectioner's sugar all over the cake to decorate.

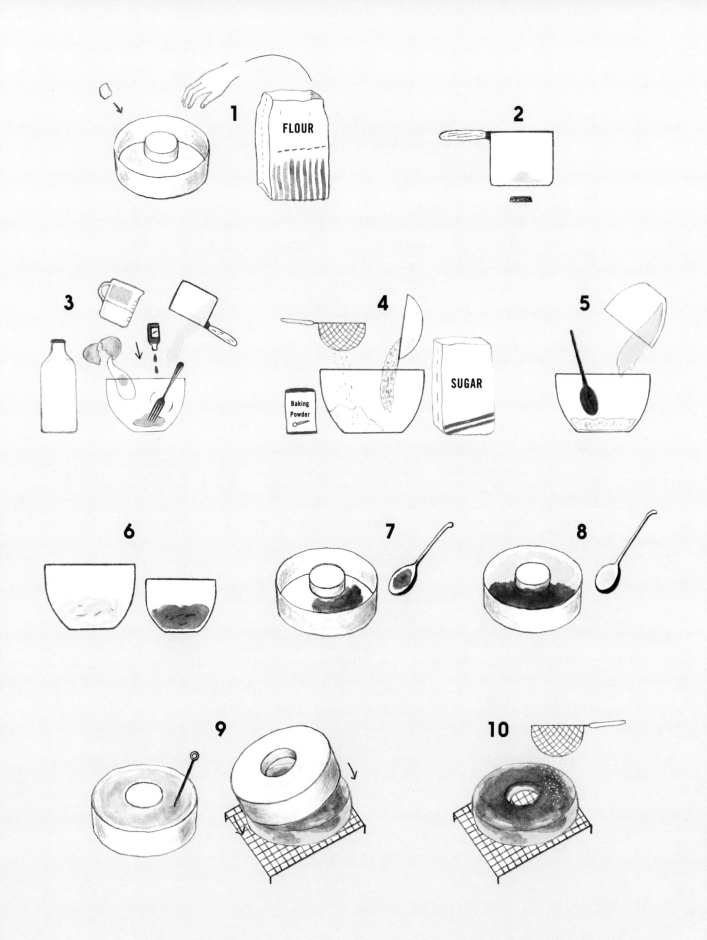

ORANGE CAKE

This cake has an amazing orange flavor. It's quite a flat cake—
it will rise in the oven, but it won't be big and tall.

SERVES	PREPARATION TIME	COOKING TIME
6−8	30 minutes	20−25 minutes

FOR THE CAKE:

7 tablespoons sweet butter,
plus extra for greasing the cake pan

—

1 orange

—

2 barnyard eggs

—

½ cup superfine sugar

—

scant 1 cup confectioner's sugar

—

scant 1 cup self-rising flour

—

½ teaspoon baking powder

FOR THE FROSTING:

scant 1 cup confectioner's sugar

—

1 orange

ORANGE CAKE

STEP 1 Turn on the oven to 350°F. Grease an 8-inch cake pan—rub a little butter all over the inside.

STEP 2 Sit the pan on a piece of baking parchment and draw around it, then cut out the round and use it to line the bottom of the pan.

STEP 3 Using the bridge technique (see pages 12–13), cut the orange in half and then squeeze the juice into a pitcher. You need about 6 tablespoons of juice, so if your orange is really juicy and has more juice than that, you could drink the rest.

STEP 4 Put the butter into a small pan and melt over gentle heat or melt in a small bowl in the microwave. Let cool.

STEP 5 Crack the eggs into a big bowl (see pages 14–15).

STEP 6 Add the superfine sugar and confectioner's sugar to the eggs and using a whisk (either a hand whisk or electric whisk) whisk until light and fluffy.

STEP 7 Stir in the cooled melted butter.

STEP 8 Sift the flour and baking powder onto the egg mixture, pour over the orange juice, and carefully mix everything together. Pour the mixture into the cake pan.

STEP 9 Using oven mitts, put the cake pan in the oven and bake for 18 minutes. To see if the cake is cooked, poke a skewer or knife into the middle—it should come out clean. If there is sticky cake mixture on the skewer, put the cake back into the oven for 3–4 minutes.

STEP 10 Using oven mitts, take the cake out of the oven. Let cool in the pan and then carefully turn the cake out onto a cooling rack so that it is the right way up.

STEP 11 Make the frosting. Using the bridge technique, cut the orange in half and squeeze out the juice (see pages 14–15). Sift the confectioner's sugar into a bowl, add the juice, and mix together.

STEP 12 Poke a few holes in the cooled cake with a skewer or a fork and then pour the frosting over the top of the cake—it will run all over the cake into the holes, down the sides, and onto the table!

HAZELNUT CAKE

This is a simple and delicious cake to make. The lemon zest
(the grated yellow rind of a lemon) adds a wonderful flavor
and the nuts give the cake texture. If you want the cake
to taste even more lemony, mix the juice of the lemon with
a little confectioner's sugar and drizzle this over the cake.

SERVES	PREPARATION TIME	COOKING TIME
6–8	30 minutes	30–35 minutes

7 tablespoons sweet butter,
plus extra for greasing the cake pan

—

1⅔ cups whole hazelnuts
(or ground almonds, to save time)

—

1¾ cups self-rising flour

—

1 cup superfine sugar

—

1 lemon

—

2 barnyard eggs

—

¼ cup milk

—

confectioner's sugar, for dusting
the top of the cake (optional)

HAZELNUT CAKE

STEP 1
Turn on the oven to 350°F. Grease an 8-inch cake pan—rub a little butter all over the inside.

STEP 2
Sit the pan on a piece of baking parchment and draw around it, then cut out the round and use it to line the bottom of the pan.

STEP 3
Put the butter into a small pan and melt over gentle heat or melt in a small bowl in the microwave. Let cool.

STEP 4
To make the hazelnuts taste even more nutty, you can "toast" them in a skillet over gentle heat. It will only take a few minutes—you don't want them to be too brown. Move them around the skillet with a wooden spoon so they don't burn.

STEP 5
Put the hazelnuts into a food processor and whizz until they are finely chopped. Ask an adult to help you with this (see pages 10–11). If you don't have a food processor, you can put the nuts in a plastic bag and bash them with a rolling pin.

If you want to save time, you can use ground almonds instead of toasting and grinding whole hazelnuts.

STEP 6
Sift the flour into a big bowl. Add the sugar and ground nuts to the flour.

STEP 7
Grate the lemon zest (see pages 14–15). Watch your fingers and keep them well away from the grater! Add the zest to the flour. Stir together and then make a well in the middle of the bowl so that you can see the bottom.

STEP 8
Crack the eggs into a pitcher (see pages 14–15). Add the cooled melted butter and milk and mix with a fork.

STEP 9
Pour the egg mixture into the well in the bowl and then carefully stir the egg mixture so that you gradually bring all the ingredients together.

STEP 10
Spoon the cake mixture into the pan. Using oven mitts, put in the oven and bake for 30 minutes. Test to see if the cake is cooked by poking a skewer into the middle. If the skewer comes out clean, the cake is cooked. If it has mixture stuck to it, put the cake back into the oven for another 5 minutes. Let cool in the pan and then carefully turn the cake out onto a cooling rack. Using a small strainer, sprinkle confectioner's sugar over the cake to decorate.

STUFFED PEACHES

Amaretti are small, dome-shaped Italian cookies made with almonds. They're very light, with a crunchy texture. These stuffed peaches are good on their own, or served with ice cream or yogurt.

SERVES	PREPARATION TIME	COOKING TIME
4	15 minutes	1 hour

1 tablespoon sweet butter

—

5 peaches

—

4 amaretti biscuits

—

2 barnyard eggs

—

2 tablespoons unsweetened cocoa powder

—

4 tablespoons superfine sugar

STUFFED PEACHES

STEP 1

Turn on the oven to 325°F. Rub a little butter all over an ovenproof dish (keep the remaining butter for later).

STEP 2

Using the bridge cutting technique (see pages 12–13), cut the peaches in half. Twist the peaches to help separate the halves.

STEP 3

Use a teaspoon to scoop out the pits. Using the claw technique (see pages 12–13), cut one of the peaches into small pieces and put into a bowl.

STEP 4

Using a teaspoon, scoop a little flesh out of the middle of all the other peach halves to help make a slightly bigger hole.

STEP 5

Put these bits of flesh into the bowl with the chopped peach.

STEP 6

Put the peach halves into the ovenproof dish with the cut side facing upward.

STEP 7

Using your hands crush the amaretti cookies into small pieces and add to the chopped peach.

STEP 8

Separate the eggs as you only need the yolks (the orange part) for this recipe. Crack the egg (see pages 14–15) onto a saucer. Then carefully put a small cookie cutter over the yolk and tilt the saucer to pour the egg white into a bowl, leaving the yolk inside the cutter on the saucer. Do the same with the other egg. Keep the egg whites to make meringues or add them to an omelet.

STEP 9

Add the egg yolks, unsweetened cocoa powder, and sugar to the amaretti cookies and peach, and mix everything together.

STEP 10

Divide the mixture among the peach halves—pile it up into a dome shape, and dot each one with a tiny bit of butter. Using oven mitts, put in the oven and bake for 1 hour. Serve hot or warm.

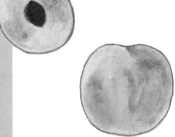

BANANA CREAM

To make this quick, easy, and deliciously creamy dessert, you need really nice ripe bananas. This recipe makes a small amount of dessert for four people. You can always increase the quantities to make more!

SERVES	PREPARATION TIME	COOKING TIME
4	5 minutes	—

2 ripe bananas, plus an extra banana
to decorate (optional)

—

½ lemon

—

4 tablespoons mascarpone cheese

—

8 tablespoons plain yogurt

—

4 teaspoons honey

—

a pinch of ground cinnamon

BANANA CREAM

STEP 1

Peel the 2 bananas and put the flesh into a bowl. Using a potato masher or a fork, mash the bananas until smooth. Cut the lemon in half using the bridge cutting technique (see pages 12–13). Squeeze the lemon juice over the bananas and mix with a fork.

STEP 2

Add the mascarpone cheese and yogurt to the mashed banana and mix together, then swirl through the honey.

STEP 3

Spoon into small serving dishes. If you like, you can put a few extra slices of banana on top to decorate. Sprinkle with a little ground cinnamon and serve.

FRUITS OF THE FOREST ICE CREAM

You don't need an ice-cream machine to make
this berry ice cream, only a freezer. It's quick
and simple, and an amazing color.

SERVES	PREPARATION TIME	COOKING TIME
6–8	3¼ hours	—

1¼ cups heavy cream

—

3¼ cups frozen berries, such as blackberries,
raspberries, redcurrants, or blackcurrants
(you will need a mixture of berries)

—

½ lemon

—

scant 1 cup superfine sugar

FRUITS OF THE FOREST ICE CREAM

STEP 1

Pour the cream into a big bowl and using a hand whisk or electric whisk, whisk it until it holds in soft peaks—when you lift the whisk out of the cream, it should look like snowy mountains! If you whisk the cream for too long, it will become too firm and stiff.

STEP 2

Put the frozen berries into a food processor. Cut the lemon in half using the bridge cutting technique (see pages 12–13). Squeeze the lemon juice over the fruit, add the sugar, and whizz until the berries are mashed up. Ask an adult to help with the food processor (see pages 10–11).

STEP 3

Spoon the mashed fruit into the whipped cream and carefully fold everything together. Spoon the mixture into a freezeproof container (a clean used ice-cream tub or other plastic container is ideal) cover with a tight-fitting lid, and freeze for 3 hours or until frozen.

INDEX

INDEX

RECIPES ADAPTED AND WRITTEN BY AMANDA GRANT

Amanda is a food writer, broadcaster, and mother of Ella, Lola, and Finley. She has published several books about healthy eating for children, writes the Junior Cooks pages for *Delicious* magazine, and is passionate about teaching children about good food and how to cook.

ILLUSTRATED BY HARRIET RUSSELL

Harriet has created many successful books for children and teenagers. She loves to cook Italian food, and particularly likes the recipe for linguine with pesto on page 94 of this book.

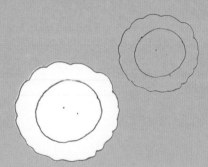

Phaidon Press Inc.
65 Bleecker Street
New York, NY 10012

phaidon.com

First published 2009
This edition 2019
© 2009, 2019 Phaidon Press Limited

The recipes in this book are adapted from *The Silver Spoon*, © 2005 Phaidon Press Limited, which was first published in Italian in 1950, eighth edition (revised, expanded and redesigned 1997) © Editoriale Domus S.p.A.

ISBN 978 1 83866 019 2 (US edition)
002-0719

A CIP catalogue record for this book is available from the Library of Congress.

Photographs by Angela Moore
Designed by Meagan Bennett

Printed in China